How Your 21st-Century Church Family Works

How Your 21st-Century Church Family Works

Understanding Congregations as Emotional Systems

Second Edition

Peter L. Steinke

Foreword by Emlyn A. Ott

An Alban Institute Book

ROWMAN & LITTLEFIELD
Lanham • Boulder • New York • London

Published by Rowman & Littlefield

An imprint of The Rowman & Littlefield Publishing Group, Inc.

4501 Forbes Boulevard, Suite 200, Lanham, Maryland 20706

www.rowman.com

86-90 Paul Street, London EC2A 4NE, United Kingdom

The author gratefully acknowledges the following: The *Saturday Evening Post* for permission to reprint the Erickson cartoon in chapter 1 (© 1978). Robert Nisbit for permission to quote from Elting E. Morison's chapter in his book *Social Change* (Basil Blackwell, 1972). HarperCollins Publishers for permission to quote from Frederick Buechner's *Telling Secrets* (1991) and Aldous Huxley's *The Devils of Loudun* (1986). Zondervan Publishing House for permission to quote from Paul Brand and Philip Yancey's *Fearfully and Wonderfully Made* (1987, © 1980).

British Library Cataloguing in Publication Information Available

Library of Congress Cataloging-in-Publication Data Is Available

Names: Steinke, Peter L., author. | Steinke, Rene, editor.
Title: How your 21st-century church family works : understanding congregations as emotional systems / Peter L Steinke ; edited by René Steinke ; foreword by Emlyn A. Ott.
Description: Second edition. | Lanham : Rowman & Littlefield, 2021. | "An Alban Institute Book." | Includes bibliographical references and index. | Summary: "Peter L. Steinke's daughter brings together the final writings from her father in this update of his classic book How Your Church Family Learns. The new edition includes a foreword from Steinke's longtime colleague Emlyn A. Ott at Healthy Congregations-the nonprofit consultancy founded by Steinke"— Provided by publisher.
Identifiers: LCCN 2021038829 (print) | LCCN 2021038830 (ebook) | ISBN 9781538149133 (pbk. : alk. paper) | ISBN 9781538149140 (electronic)
Subjects: LCSH: Parishes—Psychology. | Church controversies. | System theory.
Classification: LCC BV640 .S785 2021 (print) | LCC BV640 (ebook) | DDC 253—dc23
LC record available at https://lccn.loc.gov/2021038829
LC ebook record available at https://lccn.loc.gov/2021038830

♾ ™ The paper used in this publication meets the minimum requirements of American National Standard for Information Sciences—Permanence of Paper for Printed Library Materials, ANSI/NISO Z39.48-1992.

Contents

Foreword   vii

Preface   xi

Acknowledgments   xiii

Introduction   1

PART I: CONCEPTUALIZING EMOTIONAL PROCESSES   **5**

1   The Concept of a System   7

2   Anxiety and Reactivity   17

3   Separateness and Closeness   29

4   Stability and Change   43

5   Clarity and Compassion   57

PART II: THE CONGREGATION AS AN EMOTIONAL SYSTEM   **69**

6   Do Not Go Gently into That Glob of Glue   71

7   Being a Prophet Is Nice Work—If You Can Find a Job   83

8   What Shall It Profit a Parish If It Gets over the Hump but Falls into the Abyss?   93

9 Remembering the Future   103

10 Believing and Belonging   115

Appendix A: Systems and Implementing Change   125

Appendix B: Imagining the Future Church   127

Bibliography   131

Index   133

About the Author   141

Foreword

I met Peter Steinke at St. Malo Retreat Center in Allenspark, Colorado.

I was there to be trained as a "Bridgebuilder" facilitator, one of the applications of systems thinking that Peter had pioneered in the 1990s. I was asked to assist my denomination in leading congregations through conflict processes at the time. This was a process that I wanted to understand more deeply. That experience in the Aspens was the beginning of a trajectory in learning and engagement that I have continued for over twenty-five years. The training led to my service on the Advisory Board of the developing "Healthy Congregations" project. The project turned into a nonprofit entity that took on a life of its own, expanding beyond its "granted" birth among two Lutheran denominations to an organization that now engages with twenty-seven different denominations. I have been honored to serve this organization as Executive Director since Peter's retirement in 2006.

When I use the word training, I am not telling the whole story or really reflecting what is at the heart of the theory and practice that became Peter's life work. It is about engaging with families and communities. It is about applying the observation and research initiated by L. Murray Bowen and made real and expanded in the lives of faith communities through the application of Edwin Friedman, Israel Galindo, Larry Matthews, Ron Richardson, Margaret Marcuson, and the faculty of The Center for Family Process, where Peter first did his training with Rabbi Friedman.

Then there was Peter L. Steinke. As you can see from this updated and revised version of a classic in congregational life, Peter was working on an engagement in systems thinking and application on the morning of his death. It was his passion and an everyday part of his thinking.

Observing the dynamics of relationships in faith communities in the twenty-first century has some timeless human elements to it, including the winds of societal emotional process and reactivity. Systems thinking is about learning through and living a way of life where realistic relationships and embodied principles are at the core. Honesty and grace. It is fundamentally about understanding the human in relationship, as God has created us, and the family and faith community as an emotional unit. It also gives us some perspective on that which is automatic and that which is arising out of thoughtful, principled engagement.

Peter was a colleague, friend, and curious thinker who opened that portal for many throughout the many years of his teaching, writing, and leading. The need for a deeper awareness of systems thinking, emotional process, and application has never been clearer than in a time when we have been impacted by the opening up of the relational, physical, racial, and spiritual challenges that have existed for centuries.

During the last year of Peter's life, we were in conversation about life, ministry, family, and looking back to look forward. His thinking continued to be agile and wide-reaching at the age of eighty-two. This book is an example of his continuing curiosity about digging deeper into life and the human spirit. His realistic view of the church was always combined with connection and hope.

From young adulthood, Peter Steinke was driven to write, observe, and lead, making use of his thinking about people, families, the world, and the church. He was constantly engaging with a matrix of people who care about community, the Gospel, the poor, politics, justice, and honest engagement with reality.

The Trinity has been described as a "divine matrix." For God to be good, God can be one. For God to be loving, God has to be two, because love is always a relationship. But for God to share "excellent joy" and "delight" God has to be three, because a real community is when two persons share their common delight in a third something—together. God designed triangles into our very being.

We have been blessed by being able to think and respond more deeply to "one, two, or three" and beyond, through Peter's life and life's work. He said at one point in an email to me: "It has been a good 25 years. I am planning on coinciding my retirement with my burial."

The gifts that he has left us are these twenty-first-century observations. Timeless and timely.

Emlyn A. Ott
Executive Director, Healthy Congregations, Inc.
Associate Professor, Bexley Seabury Seminary
www.healthycongregations.com

Preface

What began as a venture in continuing education became a life-changing event for me. I met Dr. Edwin Friedman at a three-day workshop in Austin, Texas. In a conversation with him, he mentioned his new post graduate seminar in Family Emotional Process that he was leading in Bethesda, Maryland. Intrigued by his insights and style of teaching, I attended the workshop in 1988, not intending to repeat it. But the allure of the concepts and the new way of viewing the world kept me returning for nine years until Dr. Friedman's death in 1996.

In 1991, I asked him why he didn't abridge his book, *Generation to Generation*, and write a short version of it so that it could be available to more people. He saw no need to do it since the book had had multiple printings. "You," he said to me, "could write the short version." With his encouragement, I contacted the Alban Institute and *How Your Church Family Works* was written.

That was over twenty-nine years ago. There are a few things that I have changed in this second edition. One is to clarify the ways in which differentiation is how one handles oneself. Some heard the concept of "differentiation" and began to think of the "undifferentiated" people they know or have had to engage. In fact, I think Dr. Friedman would say the level of differentiation of others, especially if low, is only significant if it affects your functioning. What is primary is your own response, your own capacity to base behavior in principle, and your ability to take responsibility for your functioning.

I would also add the connection I see between "differentiation" and the "stewardship of life." They both are about managing what has been given. I hope the reader will see how self-management is crucial to the life we have been given. For we are called to be "stewards" of self and of the "emotional system" called the church.

People have reported to me that the value of the book extends beyond their lives in their congregations. The concepts have been helpful to them in other relationships and situations. What I describe as happening in congregations happens at home and at work. Another value people have acquired from the book is that when they and others now look at a circumstance or event, they do it, as one person said, "looking out the same window and standing on the same platform." They have a common way to "see" things and to understand life.

Editor's Note: Peter Steinke died on July 13, 2020, after he had made changes to the original manuscript for the second edition, but before he could add all of the new material he had planned to add. Since the first edition was published, my father continued his deep interest in neuroscience, especially as it related to systems thinking, faith, and church leadership. I've included as appendices in this edition two short chapters he had recently completed, "Systems and Implementing Change" and "Imagining Tomorrow's Church."—René Steinke

Acknowledgments

I am grateful to two teachers without whom this book would have been neither contemplated nor completed. For nine years I participated in the post graduate seminar in Family Emotional Process conducted by Dr. Edwin A. Friedman of Bethesda, Maryland. Friedman was a rabbi and family system therapist, who received immense attention from clergy and laity ever since the publication of his best-selling book, *Generation to Generation: Family Process in Church and Synagogue.* For many years Friedman studied with Dr. Murray Bowen of the Georgetown Family Center in Washington, D.C. Basing his insights on "Bowen Theory" and his own unique reflective capacity, Friedman has challenged many to think in new ways and to respond in an imaginative fashion.

Friedman was best "up close," in the give and take of his seminars. It was in these encounters that I came to understand family emotional process and to use it in my own life and work. I am fully responsible for the ideas expressed here. Any misreading or misunderstanding of Dr. Friedman's work is solely mine.

My second teacher was a group of people, not an individual. During my ten years as Director of Clergy Care for Lutheran Social Service of Texas, I counseled nearly 700 Lutheran clergy and members of their families, consulted with over 125 congregations, and conducted innumerable workshops for clergy in the state of Texas. At the same time, I addressed close to 100 clergy gatherings in 30 states. From this special position, I again learned "up close" about the disappointments and joys,

the conflicts and challenges, and the needs and hopes of clergy and congregations. They told their stories, shared their experiences, and spurred
my thinking. Those who serve and are served learn from each other.

A special note of appreciation is extended to Elmer Hohle who, after
one of my public presentations, gave me copies of several cartoons he
had drawn and subsequently has granted permission for their inclusion
in the book.

Peter L. Steinke
2020

Introduction

We think of the church in terms of biblical metaphors. It is the body of Christ, the New Israel, and shepherd and flock. Speaking personally, we use the metaphors of warmth and relationship to describe the church—a community, a family, and a gathering of caring people. Metaphorically, the church is depicted in splendor.

Moving from metaphor to reality, we may find the lustrous symbols tarnished. Congregations can exhibit bitterness, suspicion, and angry forces. Instead of zest and enthusiasm, we discover half-hearted commitment, even apathy. What we didn't expect to encounter—deception, coercion, and rejection—takes us by surprise. We find the gap between the ideal and the real disturbing. Indeed "we have this treasure in earthen vessels." The church is holy, set aside for God's purposes, and yet it is ordinary, subject to human ends.

It is not that our metaphors and ideals are false but that we fail to realize that the church functions as an emotional system. As long as people gather and interact, emotional processes occur. There are positive aspects of these processes—joy, comfort, support, cooperation, and friendship. But emotional systems are innately anxious. The downside, therefore, is the intense anxiety that distracts a congregation from its purpose, sets people at odds with each other, and builds walls against outsiders. Discussing Christian community, theologian Dietrich Bonhoeffer observed:

"There arose a reasoning among them which of them should be the greatest" (Luke 9:46). We know who it is that sows this thought in the Christian community. But perhaps we do not bear in mind enough that no Christian community ever comes together without this thought immediately emerging as a seed of discord. Thus at the very beginning of Christian fellowship there is engendered an invisible, often unconscious, life-and-death contest "There arose a reasoning among them": This is enough to destroy a fellowship. (*Life Together*, p. 90)

Our expectations of the Christian community far exceed those we hold for other communities to which we belong. So should it be. Yet, as Bonhoeffer suggested, we may not "bear in mind enough" the "invisible, often unconscious" processes that seed disruption in our midst.

Some may argue that the church's relationship system is different from the human interactions experienced elsewhere in our lives. There is the presence of the Holy Spirit and the power of the forgiveness of sin. Certainly, both distinguish the church's life. But neither negates the reality of anxiety. The church is more than its emotional processes, but it is never less than these processes. Medieval theologian Thomas Aquinas stated, "Gratia non tollit naturam," which means "Grace does not abolish nature." Grace redirects human nature. Grace offers courage in the face of human reality. That's our hope. Still, one would be hard-pressed to find examples in Scripture where we are instructed to deny our humanness. We are not asked to live an unreal life in the church. We are urged to control the powers of human nature, but that is not the same as denying their reality.

Faith and anxiety are not absolutes. That is, if you express one, you do not eliminate the other. Faith can keep company with many sets of ordinary feelings that can be handled and lived with but never removed. Those who insist on a "pure" faith unstained by human emotionality make the denial of reality a condition of faith. But the encouragement of the Scripture is to "take heart," not to take cover. We take heart because we believe that human life in its totality becomes enormously fruitful in the hands of God through the power of God's gracious promises.

The presence of anxiety in the church is a given. That's life. Ignoring its alarm or treating it lightly is not a sign of faith, much less wisdom. If anything, it is foolishness, perhaps even a signal of "little faith." Emotional processes have existed since Creation. They still affect every relationship. The key question is whether or not anxiety, so much a part of these processes, infects the relationship, bringing about discord and destruction. It is the premise of this book that we need to pay attention to and work through the presence of anxious forces in the church rather than to be surprised and rendered helpless by them, or retreat from their distressing influence, or, worse yet, protect those who spread their disease among others.

The goal of this study is to conceptualize emotional processes so that we can recognize them and, ultimately, let them serve rather than corrupt the purpose of our bonding together—"for the sake of ministry, for building up the body of Christ" (Ephesians 4:13), that "every tongue confess that Jesus Christ is Lord, to the glory of God the Father" (Philippians 2:11). Our primary dilemma is that emotional processes are difficult to observe. They are invisible, often beyond our awareness. They are even more elusive if we have no way to understand them, to make them visible. And, of course, their invisibility increases when we ourselves are involved in them.

As a way to think about and work through emotional processes, we will examine "family systems" or "systems theory." The concepts portrayed in systems thinking offer us means through which to make visible and specific what is unseen and confusing. We will see the church's life together in a different way. For system theory creates a shift in our awareness. It restructures how we think. By rethinking human interactions, we will gain access to new ways of living with one another.

The book is not about technique or "how-to"; it is about theory and observable facts. "How" things happen. It is intended to sharpen awareness of emotional processes. Understanding alone will not change these processes. But if understanding is translated into new ways of being and doing, emotional processes can be directed toward health and well-being as we live the divine vocation entrusted to us.

The church is not a family. Families are more committed and intense. Their relationships are repeatedly reinforced and deeply patterned. Nonetheless, like a family, the church is an emotional unit. The same emotional processes experienced in the family operate in the church; thus the use of the term "church family" in the title and text of the book. Looking at how the church family works as an emotional system, I address questions such as "why the church family resists taking steps toward change and growth?", "how the church family can change the way it functions?", "what the church family can do when it is threatened by its own emotional processes?", "what interactional patterns are most beneficial to its life and purpose?", and "who can most affect change and calm in its midst?".

The book is a mix of theory and case studies. It begins heavily with theory which progressively lightens as the stories begin. I recommend that readers acquaint themselves with the theory before turning to the lived events. Since systems theory involves a new language as well as a new way of thinking, I have attempted to make both user-friendly. To enliven the theory, I use actual events. To protect the integrity of the people depicted in the stories, I have changed the details, though the essential events are untouched.

The book is divided into two sections, "Conceptualizing Emotional Processes" and "The Congregation as an Emotional System." It begins with a general discussion of a system (chapter 1). The four successive chapters are discussions of emotional processes in a system: "Anxiety and Reactivity" (chapter 2), "Separateness and Closeness" (chapter 3), "Stability and Change" (chapter 4), and "Clarity and Compassion" (chapter 5).

The second half of the book illumines the theory through stories, especially chapters 6 through 8: "Do Not Go Gently into That Glob of Glue," "Being a Prophet Is Nice Work—If You Can Find a Job," and "What Shall It Profit a Parish if It Gets Over the Hump but Falls into the Abyss." Chapter 9 is a challenge to congregational leaders, both clergy and laity, to be on the side of imagination and growth. It is called "Remembering the Future."

Prior to writing the book manuscript, I offered workshops that bore the same title as the book in eleven states. The participants completed evaluation forms. Many indicated an interest in joining the theory with theological reflection. I have, therefore, inserted a chapter that views emotional processes in systems from a theological vantage point.

"Believing and Belonging" (chapter 10) is too brief, to be sure, but others have found even its brevity helpful.

With the unusually high rate of change, experienced by no previous cohort of people, our leaders may not know how to guide and challenge us as before, given the unsettling of what was little known before. I've added the new chapters, therefore, "Systems and Implementing Change" and "Imagining Tomorrow's Church."

Part I

CONCEPTUALIZING EMOTIONAL PROCESSES

Chapter 1

The Concept of a System

Every concrete thing is either a system or a component of a system, i.e., a thing composed of interconnected things.

—Mario Bunge

From cells to societies to ecosystems, things enjoy existence only by virtue of their relationships in larger wholes.

—Charles M. Johnston

TYING TOGETHER

Reality is more complex than a tidy theory. Nevertheless, a theory helps us to organize complexity. From a place of reference, we put the forces at play into a coherent pattern. We see how things are connected; we make sense of what is happening. And we become more aware of how we might respond and where we might aim our efforts.

Systems Theory is a way of conceptualizing reality. It organizes our thinking from a specific vantage point. Systems thinking considers the *interrelatedness* of the parts. Instead of seeing isolated, unrelated parts, we look at the whole. For example, a small child looking at a house from different angles sees different objects. She lives with the illusion of seeing separate pieces that do not fit together. As her perceptual mastery increases, she will recognize that the different angles of view are parts of the same house. She will observe the house as a whole.

Learning theorist Jean Piaget noted that for approximately the first fifteen years of life we assimilate pieces of information. New images and experiences enter the door of the right lobe and store themselves in the left lobe. We learn to associate what we assimilate. We see likenesses between dissimilar objects; we coordinate separate entities into interrelated parts; we realize that differences do not necessarily cancel out each other; we see how opposites are suited to one another. Looking at how things are interrelated, we reach a higher plane of thinking. We see both parts and wholes.

Systems thinking deepens our understanding of life. We see it as a rich complexity of interdependent parts. Basically, a system is a set of forces and events that interact, such as a weather system or the solar system. To think systemically is to look at the ongoing, vital interaction of the connected parts.

A favorite axiom of system proponents is "the whole is greater than the sum of its parts." Our bodies, for instance, are systems composed of many organs (lungs, heart, liver, pancreas, etc.). Together or as a whole, the body is greater than any separate organ. Likewise, a group of people is different from the individual actions of all the people combined. The whole is a force in itself. It exerts a force greater than any of its composing pieces.

AROUND AND AROUND

When we think systemically, we cannot understand one thing without the other. A and B are indivisible. Rather than thinking that A causes B, we see that A and B are mutual influences on one another. To think in terms of cause and effect is to think that things are influenced only in one direction. This is straight-line thinking. System theorys teaches us to think of loops instead of lines. A and B are both the influencer and the influenced. They are "co-causal." Every cause is an effect; every effect is a cause. We look, therefore, at how A and B *mutually maintain their interaction*, not for who causes what. (See Diagram 1.1.)

Systems thinking looks for circles of influence. Let me illustrate. Newton's apple, notorious as Adam's, brought to the forefront the law

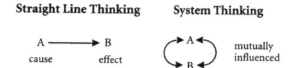

Diagram 1.1

of gravity. Because of gravitational pull, we learned that what goes up must come down. But an inquisitive person asked how the apple got up in the tree in the first place. If there is a law of gravity, he thought, might there also be a law of levity—what goes down must come up. Water, for instance, runs downhill under the influence of gravity. Yet water streams upward into the upper air as invisible vapor. There it is transformed into clouds only to fall back to earth in the form of dew or rain. Never at rest, water is part of a continuous circulatory process. We cannot understand a rain shower unless we think of the whole process. Nothing can fall if it cannot also rise. Gravity and levity mutually influence one another.

Straight-line thinking is appropriate for mechanics and physical objects. But we often mistake what happens in the world of objects for what happens in the world of living things. Theorist Gregory Bateson observed that in the physical world causality is linear. Using a billiard table as an example, he noted that one ball strikes another, causing it to move and ricochet off a third ball. One force acts upon another. But billiard balls have no response mechanisms. In the world of living things, more than mere force is involved. Action provides information. People respond or react to it. A response is a choice. It is intentional. A reaction is automatic. It is reflexive.

To illustrate the difference between what happens in the physical world and the living world, therapist Lynn Hoffman has compared the difference between kicking a stone and kicking a dog. When you kick a stone, you exert force in one direction. The stone moves relative to the force of the kick and the weight of the stone. The stone doesn't shout or demand, "Why did you kick me?" When you kick a dog, there is a counter-move. The dog may cringe and look hurt, run away, bark menacingly, or lurch forward to attack. There is now information and relatedness. The kicker may scowl, retreat, shout, or rethink his kicking behavior.

AGAIN AND AGAIN

Systems theory focuses attention on how interactions are mutually influenced and how they become *patterned* or repeated. Consider the political system. Candidates make sweeping promises that they could never possibly fulfill. The electorate wants more from their elected elders than they could actually give. The two parts are interrelated. The politician's outlandish pledge and the electorate's fanciful desires form a pattern of behavior. Their functioning is reciprocal. As the interaction is repeated, it is reinforced. Before long the pattern itself regulates the functioning of the parts. It's as if the pattern has a life of its own. We know that the candidate's espousal, "I'll do this for you," is exaggerated; we know that he'll never deliver on these puffed-up promises. Also, we realize that our expectations are magnified and beyond satisfaction. But promise and expectation form a balance, become patterned, and persist.

Established patterns are called homeostasis (literally, "to stay the same"). Physiologist Walter B. Cannon first employed the term to describe the stable working of our biological system. Our internal environment must remain fairly constant. Since slight deviations from the norm endanger our physical health, our bodies function to maintain balance. Biologically, we have homeostatic mechanisms for the maintenance of temperature, for the amount of light our eyes can tolerate, and for levels of fluids, salts, and blood sugar. We have internal means that seek the most favorable conditions for an interactive survival. To secure the stability of the organism, the body functions as a cooperative community preventing it from being overwhelmed by changing conditions or restoring the necessary balance after conditions change it.

When subjected to virus, injury, or malfunctioning organs, the body's homeostatic forces go to work. If balance is reclaimed, there is health. But if the regulating mechanisms fail to some degree—when temperature, for instance, rises and remains in a state of imbalance for too long—there is illness.

All life is marked by the continuing play of balance and imbalance. But when we turn from the internal milieu of the body to the external environment of the body politic, circumstances are more complex. Externally, we also need stabilizing forces. Keeping traditions and following rules are homeostatic forces. But slight deviations from the norm are not necessarily as life-threatening socially as biologically. Thus there is more scope for adaptation. In fact, change is necessary for

Illustration 1.1 Reprinted with permission from the *Saturday Evening Post* © 1978.

survival. Living things grow and develop. Balancing forces, however, may keep in place or within a narrow range of response what needs to be modified.

Relationship systems require stability. We develop patterns to ensure reliable and continuous interaction. Consequently, when a customary pattern is disturbed, we suffer "culture shock." Newly-weds experience it with one another as much as a visitor to a foreign country does. A new church member in California laments the loss of fixed ways, saying, 'This isn't the way we did it in Minnesota." Almost instinctively, we either resist change or reduce its shock by restoring the familiar, making a situation "like home" or "the same as in Minnesota." As we say, we are creatures of habit. We need continuity and sameness. At the same time we need to be flexible. Living things grow and develop. Therefore change is as normal as the

norms to which we become accustomed. With the passing of the honeymoon period, the early glow recedes. Reality intrudes. People have
to negotiate new ways of living together. A group's goals shift. Old
adjustments are challenged. Trauma suddenly bolts into life, forcing
individuals to alter their usual pattern of relating.

THE WHOLE ORGANIZES THE PARTS

Systems thinking instructs us to look at *how the whole is wired
together.* In a human system, the parts are arranged into a whole
through functioning positions. By functioning in a specific way, each
person contributes to the system's balance. As long as everyone functions in the same way, the arrangement is stable. For example, the
parent-child relationship is structured for the child's protection and
welfare. As the child matures and requires less parental oversight, the
parent-child interactions change. The protector and protected arrangement is altered. For some families the transition is relatively smooth.
A parent permits the child to be more self-sufficient, and the child
assumes increased control of life. In other cases the developmental
shift is tumultuous. A parent holds on to the child tenaciously, and
the child resists bitterly. Or a parent releases the reins yet the child
refuses to be self-reliant.

Relationship systems can be arranged in many ways through functioning positions. The three most common arrangements are *complementary*, *contrary*, and *similar*.

Complementary: Jack acts helpless; Jill takes care of him. Tom believes
it will rain on every parade, but Sue always looks for sunshine.
Contrary: Adam says, "Red," which means Eve will say, "Blue." Tom
detests wearing ties, and Sue buys him a new tie on every gift-giving
occasion.
Similar: If Adam says, "Red," Eve will say, "Red." Tom and Sue never
go to parades for fear of rain.

Relationships are arranged, whether it is "opposites attract" (complementary), "intimate enemies" (contrary), or "birds of a feather flock

together" (similar). The arrangements are maintained by mutual functioning but disturbed by new ways of behaving.

ALONE AND TOGETHER

Relationship systems have a unique dimension. What most distinguishes relationship systems from other systems are emotional processes. These processes are driven by and organized around two forces: the need to be separate and the need to be close. We need to be separate (to be alone, to stand on our own two feet) and to be close (to be together, to stand hand-in-hand). The two forces are in tension; they are anxiety-producing. How can you stand alone and still embrace another? How can you be close to someone and not lose your "self?" How can you go in both directions? At times the tension is frightening. Read, for example, Fredrick Buechner's description of his teenage daughter's encounter with *anorexia nervosa*:

> Young people crave to be free and independent. They crave also to be taken care of and safe. The dark magic of anorexia is that it satisfies both of these cravings at once. By not eating, you take your stand against the world that is telling you what to do and who to be. And by not eating you also make your body so much smaller, lighter, weaker that in effect it becomes a child's body again and the world flocks to your rescue. This double victory is so great that apparently not even self-destruction seems too high a price to pay. (*Telling Secrets*, p. 23)

The two opposing needs confront a young person in new and powerful ways. Yet this is not only an adolescent's issue. It pervades every stage of life. A recently widowed woman of sixty-five wrestles with accepting her aloneness and at the same time satisfying her need for support from her children. She wonders if she has withdrawn herself from them too much or if she has imposed on them too often.

Ponder the predicament of the mid-forty businessman who, facing a decline in sales, must lay off a number of employees to keep his business solvent. Among the potential pool of employees to be released is the husband of his wife's friend. Will his wife's relationship influence his decision? Will he make his decision based on an objective standard?

Then, too, think about the pastor who is a friend of a lay leader. A circumstance arises in which the pastor and the lay leader represent different viewpoints about the church budget. The pastor favors funding new programs, but the lay leader commands a group wanting to upgrade the facilities. Will the pastor risk the continued support of his friend or bow to the lay leader's position? The possibilities of such situations—the tension between separateness and closeness—are endless.

SELF-DIFFERENTIATION

Murray Bowen introduced the term *self-differentiation* to depict the capacity of maintaining the two forces in balance. Self-differentiation is

- defining yourself and staying in touch with others
- being responsible for yourself and responsive to others
- maintaining your integrity and well-being without intruding on that of others
- allowing the enhancement of the other's integrity and well-being without feeling abandoned, inferior, or less of a self
- having an "I" and entering a relationship with another "I" without losing your self or diminishing the self of the other

Self-differentiation means "being separate together" or "being connected selves." It is a life-long learning process, never attained, always tested.

Self-differentiation never happens in isolation. It requires other people. In fact, the word for "self" derives from the Latin word *se* or *seu*. It means *apart from* (cf. secede, seclude, and segregate). But it is also used in reference to connected people. Another form of *se* is *sibi* from which we have coined the words "gossip" or "sibling." *Solus* is another word stemming from *seu*, thus "solitude," "solo," and "isolate"; but also the word *socius* is a progeny of *seu*, leading to the word "social" which means liking to be with others. Both forces—separateness and closeness—are always positions vis-a-vis others, positions of dialogue, give and take, and alongsideness.

SUMMARY

Systems thinking is a way of seeing

- the whole,
- how the parts mutually influence one another,
- how the circle of influence becomes patterned, and
- how the pattern is maintained by the
  arrangement of the functioning parts.

In an emotional system there is always

- information (a reaction or a response) and
- the struggle to be self-defined and yet in touch with others.

Chapter 2

Anxiety and Reactivity

Anxiety creates its own disaster.

—Gregory Bateson

Man has always been a specifically anxious creature with an almost untapped capacity for worry; it is a gift that distinguishes him from other forms of life.

—Lewis Thomas

Anxiety cannot be avoided, but it can be reduced.

—Rollo May

ANXIOUS RELATIONSHIPS

All relationship systems become anxious. Put people together and inevitably anxiety will arise. Anxiety can be infectious. We can give it to others or catch it from them. What precisely triggers anxiety is unique to each system. Common activators are significant changes and losses. They upset the stable patterns and balance of the system.

Equally as important as to what sets off anxiety is where it is focused. Anxiety is free-floating. But eventually it drains off and settles somewhere. Relationship systems have favorite ducts and crevices for the deposit of its flow. The most vulnerable or responsible people in the relationship network are the usual targets.

Anxiety can be the ruin or the salvation of our relationships. It is an alarm mechanism. It alerts us to potential danger. But sometimes it goes off too often or quickly. Sometimes we do not seem able to regulate it. Shocked, we lash out, hold our ground, or retreat. Furthermore, anxiety makes transparent what is not alike. Even more, it magnifies differences. "Differing" can be a synonym for discord. Based on a certain type and degree of agreement and commonality, relationships are threatened by separateness, differentiation, and diversity. Anxiety affects most adversely the relationship systems that have little capacity to tolerate or manage differences. Still, anxiety can be our deliverance. It has motivational power. Anxiety provokes change. It prods and pushes us toward innovation or transformation. If, however, it reaches a certain intensity, it prevents the very change it provokes. What is stimulus becomes restraint. We "lose our head" or "cool," as we say, essentially our awareness and composure; we are too reactive to be responsive.

THREE-IN-ONE

With anger and anguish, anxiety shares the same Latin root word—*angere*. It is translated "to choke" or "to give pain by pushing together." The noun form of the verb is *angustus*, meaning "narrow." Anxiety is emotional pain. It constricts and limits life. At the center of its painfulness is uncertainty. We can neither put our finger on what is disturbing us nor pick out a clear-cut villain who is threatening us. Nothing in specific stimulates it, and nothing in particular is its object. Anxiety diminishes clarity and objectivity. It interferes with our capacity to think creatively. We cannot stand outside of the vague dread and observe it. We do not know what we are afraid of, what terrifies us. In contrast to fear, anxiety is undifferentiated. It has no definite focus. We speak of agoraphobia (the fear of open spaces) and claustrophobia (the fear of enclosed spaces). But anxiety is an imprecise warning signal. It has no object, yet continues to scream warning.

Because anxiety affects our thinking capacities, we need to observe the working of the human brain. Most helpful is neurologist Paul MacLean's discussion of the "triune brain." The architecture of the brain is three-tiered (see Diagram 2.1).

At the base of the brain, where the central nervous system connects with the brain stem, is the reptilian brain. Above it lies the mammalian

A Schematic Cross Section of the Human Brain

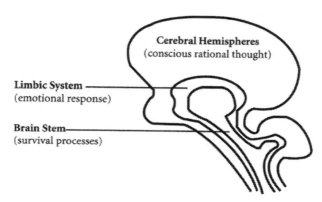

Diagram 2.1

brain, sometimes called the limbic system. The largest brain area, the third layer, is the neocortex or cerebral hemispheres. Each brain has its own function, though the three function as one.

THE BRAIN AT WORK

The reptilian brain regulates *automatic* processes such as circulation and respiration. It functions regularly and continuously. Its mechanisms are biologically designed for the protection and survival of the organism. Suppose, for instance, you are driving your car. Your thoughts drift away from traffic conditions. Suddenly and without conscious thought, you depress the brake pedal with your foot. Sensing danger, the reptilian brain acts instinctively. Take into account another situation. You are conversing with a family member who brings up a painful topic. You change the subject. Immediately and unconsciously you defend yourself against discomfort. You are using the automatic processes of the reptilian brain as a way to adapt to threats.

The second tier of brain matter regulates behavior that includes playing, nurturing, bonding, and flocking, as well as emotive expressions such as shock and repugnance, sorrow, and rejoicing. The mammalian brain also operates without premeditation. Research indicates that this part of the brain plays a mediating role between pleasure-pain, tension-relaxation, and fight-flight. At times, however, the limbic system can run away, oscillate, or "go haywire." Instead of maintaining balance, it tilts toward one of the pairs of opposites, destabilizing equilibrium. Mutual restraint is lost. For example, a tennis player enjoys the game despite frustrating moments. After several horrible games, the player's disgust becomes overpowering. She vows to give up the game and never play again. Her pain has run away from her pleasure.

The reptilian and mammalian brains compose 15 percent of the brain mass. They are well connected by neurons. Involved with involuntary responses, they operate "like clockwork." But being automatic, they cannot be inventive; being reactive, they cannot be creative. They are slaves to precedent and strangers to novelty. Yet who would want the section of the brain that controls respiration to be original? Imagine the left lung suggesting to the right lung, "Let's be creative and do the heartbeats in tune with the drumbeats."

The cerebral hemispheres encompass 85 percent of the brain mass. The supreme tier processes concepts, symbols, and insights. It is associated with voluntary movements. Neocortical thinking, therefore, is adept at learning new ways to cope and at imagining alternatives. Unlike the many links connecting the two lower areas of the brain, the neocortex's links to either one are sparse. Instinct and intention lack special connectedness. I've wondered if this is what Paul meant when he said that the good he intended, he didn't do, but what he detested, he did. Instinct overwhelmed intentionality.

A simple way to distinguish the parts and functions of the triune brain is noted below:

thinking cap   analyze, reflect, symbolize, observe, create
(neocortex)
house of emotion   love, hate, bond, play
(mammalian)
automatic pilot   survive, act without thinking
(reptilian)

TWO PROCESSES

Humans share the reptilian brain with lizards, snakes, and crocodiles. The mammalian brain is shared with dogs, cats, and horses. In humans the reptilian and the mammalian brains are superior to the same structures in other species. Lizards don't care for their young. They don't make playful pets. Essentially they don't "have the brains for it." Although a lizard possesses a cortex, it is so incomplete that the creeping creature adapts poorly to new circumstances. Dogs, on the other hand, can be taught new tricks. Their neocortex is larger than the lizard's.

It is said that "animals are not moved by what they cannot react to." In other words, they behave automatically. Human beings, however, are both instinctive and thoughtful. We behave as self-preserving and problem-solving creatures. The two self-preserving parts of the brain are not inferior to the thinking part merely because we share them with lesser species. They contribute to life. But they are limited. They cannot embrace the neocortex, whereas the neocortex can hold subjective states (instinct and emotion) in awareness. If the neocortex ignores the other two brains, much of the color and warmth of life is forfeited. Yet, as the center of language, imagination, and speech, the neocortex enables us to be more than a collection of reflexes. We can reflect on what is happening (insight) and plan for what might happen (foresight). The neocortex enables us to be conscious of our own inner experience and to observe outer events. We can be responsive.

lower brain
(automatic processes)
 –to defend
 –to discharge
 –to preserve
 –to react

hemispheric brain
(thinking processes)
 –to define
 –to discriminate
 –to create
 –to respond

NEGATIVE OUTCOMES

Moved by gusts of anxiety, we experience what Friedman has called a "reptilian regression." We are reactive. Automatic processes take charge:

* impulse overwhelms intention
* instinct sweeps aside imagination
* reflexive behavior closes off reflective thought

- defensive postures block out defined positions
- emotional reactivity limits clearly determined direction.

At the onset of threat, self-preservation has more relevance for survival than self-awareness. Long before we could ever talk or think, we called on automatic processes for survival. We call on them again and again. Besides, they act faster than the thinking processes. When we are anxious, we act before we think. The Automatic Pilot joins forces with the House of Emotion and dominates. In a reptilian regression our behavior is not mediated through the neocortex. Anxious, we are apt to lose objectivity and civility. We are in a position to be neither responsible nor loving. Reason and love are best served in time of calm.

In periods of intense anxiety, what is most needed is what is most unavailable—the capacity to be imaginative. Again, this is as true in the church family as in all relationship systems. Threatened, any of us may dispense with our Christian convictions and values. Anxiety is no respecter of belief systems. It is an indiscriminate trigger. Threat is threat. The reptilian brain is not impressed by the sincerity of what we believe to be true; it does what it is designed to do: react instinctively.

I don't know the source of the following anecdote, but I have seen it in a couple of editorials. Called "The Lesson," the account illustrates the reactive, defensive posture of a reptilian regression.

The Lesson

Then Jesus took his disciples up the mountain and gathering them around him, he taught them:

"Blessed are the poor in spirit, for theirs is the kingdom of heaven,
Blessed are the meek,
Blessed are they that mourn,
Blessed are the merciful,
Blessed are they that thirst for justice,
Blessed are you when persecuted,
Blessed are you when you suffer,
Be glad and rejoice for your reward is great in Heaven."
Then Simon Peter said,
    "Are we supposed to know this?"
And Andrew said,
    "Do we have to write this down?"

And James said,
   "Will we have a test on this?"
And Philip said,
   "I don't have any paper."
And Bartholomew said,
   "Do we have to turn this in?"
And John said,
   "The other disciples didn't have to learn this."
And Matthew said,
   "May I go to the boys' room?"
And Judas said,
   "What does this have to do with real life?"
Then one of the Pharisees who was present asked to see Jesus's lesson plan and inquired of Jesus, "Where is your anticipatory set, and your objectives in the cognitive domain?"
And Jesus wept.

SITUATIONAL OR HABITUAL

Two types of anxiety must be distinguished. Each leads to different results. Anxiety may be *acute* or *chronic*. Acute anxiety is crisis generated. It is situational or time-based. For instance, we are suddenly irritated or jolted by some event. At first we are like a rider who gets on his horse and rides off in all directions. Later we gain self-control. We steer our horse back to the trail. In the church family, acute anxiety may mount when there are budgetary difficulties, polarizing political differences, the loss of a pastor, a building program, an influx of new members, or significant change in lay leadership.

Chronic anxiety is habitual. We can't put anxiety to rest. Even the slightest change or a trivial annoyance incites reactive behavior. Social psychologist Carol Tavris has said that in chronic anxiety "the human chime mechanism chimes too often, as if a drunk carillonneur couldn't keep his hands off the church bells." No longer is anxiety an occasional warning signal. Rather, it is structured into life. Someone *has* anxiety if acute; someone *is* their anxiety if chronic. The automatic alarm, meant to be temporary, becomes perfunctory. Some church families, unfortunately, are chronically anxious. Chronically anxious church families may have small groups splinter off periodically. Or the family stays intact but is submissive to a small but manipulative power group. In other chronically anxious church families, leadership changes rapidly, or change is always stalled and agents of change are punished.

How can we distinguish between acute and chronic anxiety? Jesus told a story about a family, a father and his two sons. It portrays some of the differences between anxiety that is situational and habitual. The younger son emotionally distances from his family. He travels to a far country and wastes his inheritance. A great famine arises. Bereft of friends and fortune, the son finds himself knee-deep in feeding pigs. Imagine, the shame of it all. Still, he comes to his senses. He has enough capacity to manage his adversity and to use his imagination: "I'll offer myself to my father as a servant." He returns home. Before the younger son reaches the house, his father's joy is already bursting into gracious gestures—a ring, a robe, a pair of sandals, and a centerpiece for his homecoming celebration, a fatted calf. Hearing the noise, the older brother leaves the field and is at the back door inquiring about the boisterous activity. When he discovers that his brother has returned, he broods. We, of course, sympathize with the super-responsible firstborn. Without his work there never would have been a fatted calf to kill. Nonetheless, we hear this son's chronic anxiety: "These many years have I served you, and I never disobeyed your command." Unsure of his father's love, he thought that he could keep his father close by being "the good kid." Angry, he slashes at his father with a sharp complaint. "You never sacrificed as much as a goat and barbecued it for my friends and me." Chronic anxiety may show up in thoughtless obedience as well as mindless outbursts. Chronically anxious people, like the older son, keep their focus on others. They are easily and quickly hurt. They see themselves as victims. Yet, as Simone Weil has said, "It is better to say, 'I'm suffering,' than to say, 'This landscape is ugly.'"

Acutely anxious people regain their perspective. There is a return to the Thinking Cap. They have the capacity to control their reactivity. But the chronically anxious have immense difficulty keeping their hands off their own chimes. They are not self-regulating. And they are not imaginative. Note how the father appeals to his oldest son's thinking capacity: "It is fitting to rejoice and give thanks. After all, my son— your brother—was lost and is found. Son, everything I have is yours." There is no response.

Typical of chronically anxious people, the older son resorts to *either/ or* thinking. It was either "favor me" or "favor your other son"; it was all these years of obedience versus the irresponsible behavior of the other son. Anxiety-driven reactivity inhibits the use of the Thinking Cap. With little capacity for discernment, the chronically anxious reduce everything to all or nothing. Lines are drawn. It is no wonder, then, that they *overfocus* on others and their weaknesses. They blame or falsely criticize. The older son, for example, diagnoses his brother—reckless, careless, foolish. By overfocusing on the riotous brother, he is no longer responsible for his own reactive position nor responsive to his brother. To the older brother, the trouble is external to himself. Obviously, the brother cannot think systemically. For when you see yourself as part of all relational transactions, you look in both directions. You understand that in emotional systems everything is mutually influenced.

The parable of Jesus also clues us to another characteristic of chronic anxiety. There is *willfulness*. "If it's not done my way, I'll show you." Thus the older son refuses to join the festive party. If the chronically anxious cannot diminish or eradicate their pain by blaming, they'll rid themselves of it nonetheless through other means. "I'll make you suffer yet." If differences cannot be tolerated, they are likely to be persecuted.

It is the chronically anxious individuals in the church family who are apt to conduct a "search and destroy mission." They impose their wills on others. They make hostages of their gifts, attendance, and participation. They employ their stewardship as brinkmanship. Their ultimate threat is to run away from home—transferring or terminating their membership if an action is not rescinded, a person is not removed, or a demand is not satisfied. These tactics are effective in church families that place a premium on peace and harmony. They will exchange integrity for tranquility. They cannot free themselves from the bondage of others.

Basically, chronically anxious people have a low threshold for pain. This is why they are in the forefront of the effort to secure immediate relief. They hanker for answers and comfort. Threatened, they make demands, spread rumors, exaggerate circumstances, claim injustice—whatever it takes to lessen their anxiety. Governed by instinct rather than insight, they cannot be stopped by reasoning or appeasing. Mistakenly, those who must deal with them think being "nice" to the chronically anxious will earn cooperation in return. Or that being reasonable will get the reactive forces to follow suit. But the reptilian brain does not respond to nice behavior, clear thought, or sugar and roses. Under the siege of the Automatic Pilot, thoughtful and careful approaches are ignored. For this reason, too, difference itself is not the cause of the friction. Differences are problematic in proportion to the automatic processes. With the chronically anxious, the contentious issue is not at the basis of their reactivity. Even if the issue changes, their chimes are still ringing. They keep adding emotional fuel to the fire.

THE VICIOUS CIRCLE

Anxiety is not necessarily harmful to relationship systems. In fact, anxiety has the potential to transform relationships beneficially. When intense anxiety explodes into reactive behaviors and is mutually reinforced, however, a vicious circle forms. A person becomes anxious (Anxiety 1). Feeling insecure, the person reacts (Reactivity 1). In the face of the initial person's anxious reactivity, a second person becomes anxious (Anxiety 2) and reactive (Reactivity 2). (See Diagram 2.2.)

If anxious reactivity continues to be fed in both directions, it is reinforced and maintained. The individuals become unbending (Rigidity). It's as if each side says to the other, "You do it your way, I'll do it God's way." Once inflexible, people polarize. But polarity itself is anxiety-producing. The vicious circle is in place: anxiety—reactivity—rigidity—polarity—more anxiety. As long as there is a mutual "charge," the circuitry operates. (See Diagram 2.3.)

Everyone's pain is locked into the system, and everyone stays stuck together in a circular flow. Until someone frees themselves from the loop or someone else from outside the emotional circle intervenes into the feedback pattern, the chain reaction repeats and perpetuates itself.

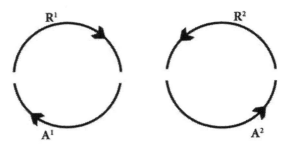

Diagram 2.2

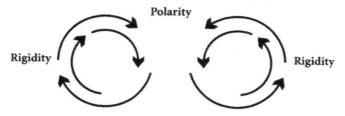

Diagram 2.3

At times a relationship system becomes aware of the anxiety-generating forces, yet refuses to use its strengths and resources to deal with the agitation. Sweeping the anxious reactivity under the rug, the system proceeds as usual. But "benign neglect" only reinforces malignant processes. Moreover, ignoring is as reactive as placating or attacking. *Vicious circles can only be disabled through exposure.* They are enabled by secrecy and avoidance.

The church family's relationships are no exception to anxiety. It was as true in the early church as it is in the contemporary church. In the book of Acts, for instance, the people gathered together in Jesus's name, "were of one heart and soul," and "had everything in common" (Acts 3:32). But a dispute threatened the equanimity. The Hellenists complained against the Hebrews because their widows were neglected in the daily distribution (Acts 6:1). At the church in Corinth more than a bipartisan spirit was present. The people splintered into contentious groups (I Corinthians 1:11–13). In the book of Jude, there is reference to the presence of "grumblers, malcontents, following their own passions, loudmouthed boasters" (Jude 16). It is no wonder that the apostle Paul warned against "enmity, strife, jealousy, anger, selfishness, dissension" (Galatians 5:20), "grumbling and questioning" (Philippians 2:14), and "godless chatter" (I Timothy 6:20). Obviously members of the first Christian communities had to contend with both bickering groups and, individually, their own anxiety.

In the Hebrew Scriptures the same peevishness is evident. The Israelites murmured against the Lord. "How long," the Lord responded, "must I tolerate the complaints of this wicked community" (Numbers 14:27).?

Meanwhile Moses was caught in the cross fire. The people "raised an outcry" against him—"Why have you brought us out of Egypt with our children and our herds to let us die of thirst?" (Exodus 17:3). The protest started when the people of God, nostalgic for their Egyptian diet spiced with garlic and sweetened with melon, became hungry in the wilderness. God sent manna. They gathered it up excitedly, were content and grateful. But they soon became weary of the same food and vigorously showed their displeasure. As people do when times are hard, they expressed their bitterness—"We loathe this worthless food" (Numbers 21:5).

The Hellenists, the Corinthians, and the Israelites prefigure the same anxious reactivity that occurs in today's church. There is conflict. Enemy camps form. The battle for the Bible, the soul, the truth, the worship style, the use of the kitchen—you name it—begins. "Church fight" sounds like an oxymoron. Where's the love, joy, and peace we expect from people there? But what happens in the church is *natural*. It is what happens in all relationship systems. Regardless of the context, emotional processes are the same. In fact, these processes become more intense when we are dealing with what lies close to the heart and the meaning of life. When we invest ourselves significantly in a relationship system, emotionality rises to the surface quickly and forcefully. Congregational skirmishes may be even more abusive than those that take place in less emotionally charged groups. Furthermore, we expect harmony to prevail in the church family, more so than in other relationship systems. Anxiety tests the supreme values of faith and love. It questions our very existence and purpose. Consequently we may fail to notice how profoundly anxiety is affecting us, either ignoring its corrupting influence or sweeping it aside too easily.

Chapter 3

Separateness and Closeness

Let him who can not be alone, beware the community. . . . Let him who is not in community, beware of being alone.

—Dietrich Bonhoeffer

What is most characteristically human about us is the tension between the desire to be "free"—self-identifying and self-choosing—and to be "related"—to love and be loved.

—Paul Tillich

In love two solitudes protect and touch and greet each other.

—Rainer Maria Rilke

IN CREATION'S SHADOW

"In the beginning God created the heaven and the earth. And the earth was without form, and void" (Genesis 1:1, 2). Everything was a purplish haze, a shapeless hulk. The air mingled with the water; the sky blended with the earth. No one could distinguish cold from hot, hard from soft, wet from dry. It was impossible to detect the runner from the race or the dancer from the dance. With everything thrown together, confusion covered the land. "And darkness was upon the face of the deep" (Genesis 1:3).

When God separated one thing from another, the formless mass took shape. God set boundaries between the land and the sea, the day and the night. Out of the undifferentiated mess came order and stability. Things were separated and assigned their territory. Still, creation remained unfinished. To the creature, the Creator delegated the task of naming things. In Eden there were no name tags, monograms, or telephone directories. Everything was generic. Adam sorted things out—"This is horse, that is cow." With the power of naming, Adam differentiated specific objects. No longer would apples be mixed with oranges. He was Adam, his companion Eve. He could note the difference between red and green; he could make comparisons between wood and stone. When things are identified, defined, and classified, they stand out and become distinctive.

As the Genesis story unfolds, the process of separating one thing from another continues. Two people join together and form a new unit. But as anyone in a modern relationship knows, the question is always which one. No doubt, the first couple had to struggle with their attempts to engulf each other. Perhaps each tried to convert the other to their own way of thinking and doing, to incorporate what was unfamiliar into their own range of familiarity.

BETWEEN BLUR AND BOUNDARY

In the Genesis story of creation, we see the foreshadowing of the drama of human development—learning to be separate yet close. An infant enters a world of "universal oneness." Nothing separates an infant from what she perceives. Her awareness is diffuse. The infant's perception is "without form, and void." Having no capacity to name and make distinctions, the newborn's world is "a big buzzing, blooming confusion" (William James). No differences exist. There are no specific persons, concrete objects, or clear boundaries.

Living in a psychological soup, the small child's development depends on her ability to differentiate between "me" and "not me," to learn where she begins and ends and others begin and end. The child needs to discern what is inside and what is outside. Although the child is physically separated from the enveloping womb of her mother, she still experiences the world as undifferentiated. To an infant, for example, her hunger and mother's nipple are one and the same. Playing on the words "mother" and "child," systems therapist

Salvador Minuchin has referred to the infant as "mochild" or "cho-ther." Because she has no ability to sort out and discriminate, the baby's world is "Mommy and I are one." Gradually, a small child experiences hints of separateness alongside encompassing together-ness. A toddler begins to explore the world on her own and then returns for the caregiver's nurturing. Later the youngster engages the yearnings of separateness and closeness when she insists on performing a task independent of daddy, nonetheless wanting his admiration. Capable of even greater separateness during adolescence, she expands her world of ideas, activities, and relationships, only now she seeks recognition from a wider audience. In adulthood she pursues intimacy with a loved one while still taking the opportunity to develop her own interests apart from her partner. Each stage of development challenges her in new ways to be apart and a part of. She will create and recreate her life-space in a lifelong process.

DRIVING FORCES

To be separate and to be close are basic needs. One is personal, the other is relational. A major task of our life is to be able to shift from one to the other with some degree of balance between the two. We need "wings" to launch into life on our own, to feel "free as a bird." We need to activate our uniqueness, our sense of "self." Furthermore, we need "roots" to hold us in place, to feel "at home." We need to connect with others, have a sense of belonging.

To separate is to take a part out of a whole. It is to give something a certain space and particular definition. Apart from an "interpenetrating mix-up," we become visible and identifiable. We exist. Literally, the verb "to exist" means "to stand out from." But separation is something created for more than isolation. We exist to be distinct from others, not distant from them. Without separateness we cannot know diversity, creativity, or longing. We separate in order to unite. We become distinct so that we can connect. Community means two unique people meet, not two fuzzy people merge. This is the fundamental idea conveyed by the word "relate." It bears the notion of "carrying back." We reach out and are reached. In a relationship what is separate is brought back. Genuine separateness is differentiation within a relationship. It's stand-ing out from others, not over against them. To stand aloof is *emotional distance*. Likewise genuine closeness is always chosen; it is not driven, forced, or obligated togetherness. Two people swallowing one another is not a relationship. It's *emotional fusion*.

FORCE + ANXIETY = EXTREME

The two needs of life—separateness and closeness—are opposites. They are forces in tension; they can be anxiety-producing. The more intense anxiety becomes, the more extreme our functioning positions will be. Either we become too remote or too entangled. If we are too anxious about being close, we disengage. We exaggerate separateness. "I can only count on myself." "I'm absolutely right." Intolerant of closeness, isolators cut off. In the same manner, if we are overanxious about being separate, we enmesh with one another. We are stuck together in an exaggerated way. "I can't live without you." "I'll give you what you want for my own peace of mind." We can't tolerate difference. We confuse closeness with sameness. But a psychic clump is not a community anymore than a cool, detached person is a self. "All extremism inevitably fails because it consists in excluding, in denying all but a single point of the entire vital reality," Spanish philosopher Ortega Gasset notes, "But the rest of it, not ceasing to be real because we deny it, always comes back and back, and imposes itself on us whether we like it or not."

FUNCTIONING POSITIONS

Bowen's concept of self-differentiation includes both forces in balance. The ideal of self-differentiation is to define self to others, stay in touch with them, and, even though there is tension between the two positions, manage whatever anxiety arises. This is not an easy accomplishment, for when we are anxious, we are more instinctive. We are pulled toward one of the extremes—emotional distance or fusion. We are therefore less self-choosing and self-directing. We have less capacity to distinguish between thought and feeling. Anxiety throws us into a state of emotional survival. We are less capable of hearing and seeing without coloring what we observe to fit our feelings. When feelings take over, distortion and misconceptions occur. Even when we "intellectualize" or "hide" our feelings, anxiety is at the helm of our life. It is a situation of feelings controlling the self.

The series of diagrams below are designed as a means for conceptualizing the two forces and the functioning positions that develop. (See Diagrams 3.1–3.4.)

Everyone must balance to some degree the two opposing forces. Ironically, people who have a good sense of their separateness will enjoy their closeness more. They are able to let down their boundaries, draw close, and pull back to reinstate their boundaries.

Diagram 1 — Centered Balance

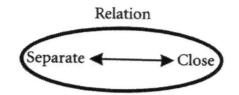

Diagram 3.1

Diagram 2 — Extreme Edges

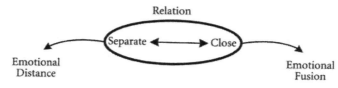

Diagram 3.2

Diagram 3 — Functioning Positions

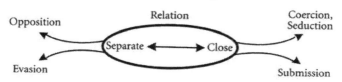

Diagram 3.3

Diagram 4 — Healthy Functioning

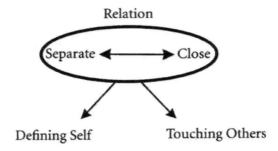

Diagram 3.4

As anxiety increases, people push toward one of the extremes, distance or fusion, to alleviate their tension. Movement toward an extreme position is primarily automatic.

Cutting off from others has an active and a passive side—opposition or evasion of them. Clinging to others also can be active (coercion or seduction) or passive (submission).

TOUCHING OTHERS

Less anxious people can tolerate the tension and manage it. Instead of cutting off or clinging to others reactively, they respond with defining the self and staying connected.

The diagrams illustrate ways in which we might function. In different settings or with various people, our functioning positions might change. We might, for instance, fuse with our children but distance from our spouse.

To further describe what these functioning positions are like, I have listed their core characteristics in table 3.1.

We all experience anxiety about separateness and closeness. Not all of us react with the same intensity or manage anxiety in the same way. But the more anxious we are, the more automatically we function. When we manage our anxiety, it becomes a springboard rather than a shotgun. We are more thoughtful, objective, and clear about our goals. We therefore function with more resiliency. At the extreme, we exclude possible adaptations. There's no full range of functioning.

Table 3.1

Cutting Off	Defining Self	Touching Others	Clutching Others
Reactive	Intentional	Spontaneous	Reactive
Automatic	Chosen	Playful	Automatic
Emotionally driven	Objectively aware	Emotionally expressive	Emotionally driven
Dependent	Responsible for self	Responsive to others	Dependent
Aggressive or defensive about keeping distance	Self-directed action	Trusting exchange	Aggressive or defensive about embeddedness
Unaware of one's need for others	Aware of self	Aware of others	Unaware of one's need for others
Stiff, rigid boundaries	Flexible boundaries (able to reinstate after loosening them)	Boundaries flexible in play, self-forgetfulness	Soft, porous boundaries
Overfunctioning to achieve self-sufficiency	Functioning for self	Allowing others to function for themselves	Overfunctioning to achieve togetherness
Minimal support, feedback, or encouragement from others	Self-respect	Respect for others; allows others to be themselves	Forces others to be like self or allows others to force one's self to be like them
Difference gained over against others	Defines self from within	Defines self to others	Differences are unacceptable; relationships defined by sameness
Narrow goals	Clearly defines goals for self	Clearly defines relationship goals	Vague, nebulous goals

THE ONGOING STORY

Someone born in a remote part of China will have a different formation experience from a person who is the offspring of a cosmopolitan family in France or an indigenous family in Mexico. The person who emerges from each of these upbringings will possess an entirely different collection of memories, observe different customs, and live a different lifestyle. We are who we are because of our history. We were welcomed and nurtured by a distinct family. We were catechized into an inherited worldview. Each of us must say,

> I am who I am because I am the child of this pair of parents, grew up at a certain period of time and with a certain group of siblings, lived in a specific neighborhood, attended school A and not B, worked in a particular job, resided in this place and not somewhere else, established a special circle of friends, experienced these events rather than those.

The self that we have is forged in a particular community. Take away our history and not much is left of us.

Long before we ever encounter the forces of separateness and closeness, past generations have been dealing with them for better or for worse. When we enter the generational stream, these forces have been at play among our predecessors. We are not born into a vacuum but onto a stage. The drama has been enacted for millennia, shaping the story that we are about to live. We can't abolish the cast of characters, the stage props, or the plot we inherit. The setting is set. We are always inheritors of the history of generations. To the philosopher's words, "Know yourself," we must add the phrase, "in the context of your family and the generations before."

Some families believe the external world is unreliable and fearsome. They make the home into a monastery with its shades down. Others find such confinement stifling. Some families develop closeness in play. Others stay emotionally connected by hostility. Claude's family keeps in touch. Claudia's family maintains loose, sporadic ties. One family rewards creativity; the other, conformity. On one side of the street, rituals are part of the family's bonds. Across the street communal rites succumb to private rights. Some families hand their children scripts of mercy: "Be who you are. We will be there when you need us." Others, though, troubled by closeness, say, "Be who you are, but don't bother us." And some give the child a script for fusion: "Be there for us, and we will love you." No matter who the cast is, what the plot reveals, or where we are slotted in the scheme of things, we are all products of families. The ongoing story is still to be told as each of us shapes the things that have shaped us.

THE GENERATIONAL TORCH

Like runners in a relay race, we pass the torch of emotional processes from generation to generation. Using a genogram—a visual outline of how a family is structured and functions—we can learn about the capacities of families to regulate their anxiety in the face of the tension between separateness and closeness. In Diagram 3.5, I have constructed an abbreviated genogram of a biblical family, including four generations.

1. Family Structure

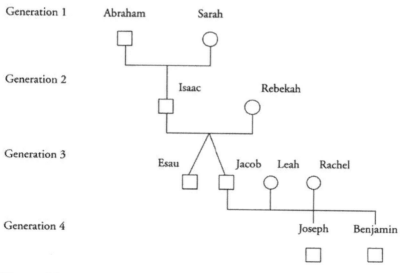

Diagram 3.5

From the details of this story in the Hebrew Scriptures, we see the forces of separateness and closeness operating through each generation. Cutoff and fusion are prominent. Generating these emotional processes are positions family members take with one another. One role transmitted from generation to generation is the family hero or chosen child. It begins with the long-awaited Isaac born to aging parents who dote upon their "treasure." In turn, the favored Isaac becomes devoted to Esau, the older of his twin sons, leaving the younger Jacob to be mother's child. Meanwhile Jacob's focus is riveted on his two sons born to his "true love" Rachel.

Overfocus leads to emotional fusion. For example, Sarah cradles Isaac all his life. Upon her death Isaac is drenched in grief. He is still mourning her death three years later. Abraham chooses Rebekah to be Isaac's wife, hoping she will be his consoler. But Isaac emotionally withdraws from her and makes Esau the apple of his eye. Counteracting, Rebekah over-attaches with Jacob.

Jacob is hardly an impressive figure, always being what someone else wants him to be. Too dependent on his mother's approval, he succumbs to her shrewd manipulation and later to her brother Laban's similarly cunning behavior. Jacob is over-engaged with his mother, so much so that when he leaves home he restages the fusion and falls in love with the first woman he meets.

We also see what happens so often in relationship systems when people fail to maintain adequate balance between separateness and closeness. People resort to secrecy, intrigue, and sabotage. For example, Rebekah and Jacob scheme to defraud Esau of his birthright. Getting a taste of his own medicine of deceit, Jacob is tricked into working an additional seven years before Laban will give him the hand of Rachel. Then Jacob's own sons, jealous of the special place of honor Joseph holds among the children, sell Joseph to slave traders, yet tell their father that Joseph was killed. (See Diagram 3.6.)

The more undifferentiated or emotionally stuck together people are, the more triangles appear. Even a cursory glance at the diagram will reveal these triangles. As the emotional tension is shifted between two members of the family to one of them and a third party, we see that there are two insiders and one outsider (cf. pages 52 through 57 for further discussion of triangles).

2. Family Functioning

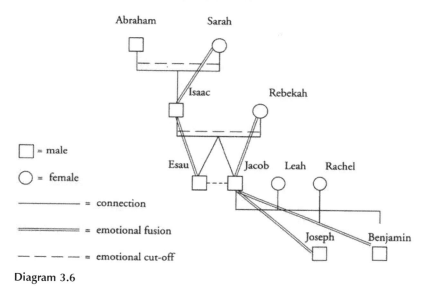

Diagram 3.6

BEYOND DYSFUNCTION

The generations of Abraham, Isaac, and Jacob do not exhibit dysfunction only. There is healing power, especially when one member of the family self-defines and stays in touch with others. Jacob frees himself from the shackles of Laban and resolves to face his brother Esau. The older twin moves beyond his early hurt and welcomes his younger brother. Joseph too restores his betraying brothers through forgiveness.

Families have restorative powers. This needs special underscoring. Our current preoccupation with family dysfunction, victimization, and pathology skews our perception of the family. The truth is that we constantly influence each other, that we leave our mark on each other's souls, that we either *hurt* or *help* each other. The psyche takes notes on all of it. Yet the studies of researcher Steve Wolin indicate that 80 percent of the children of alcoholics do not become alcoholics.

Furthermore, 60 percent of the children of child abusers do not repeat the same destructive patterns. True, the children may convert the parents' damaging behavior into other kinds of inappropriate functioning. What interests Wolin, though, is the development of *resiliency* in these children despite their parents' reactivity. A victim mentality is not the only possible outcome of family "craziness." Even though their parents function in extreme ways, some children learn to function with greater balance and flexibility. They use insight, creativity, and imagination to gain sufficient distance from the family "stuckness." Certainly they are affected by it, but they are not infected with it. Being resilient, they turn from being causative to responsive, from "Why have they done this to me?" to "What can I do about the matter?" A damage or deficit model of family interaction concentrates on the devastating conditions of life together. It ignores the challenge these very conditions provide: the challenge to increase one's capacity to be responsive and resourceful. No family or relationship can change and heal when focused on damage and blame. Reactivity is not the cure for reactivity. It simply enables it. Relationship systems regain their balance when they become imaginative instead of automatic and instinctive.

CHURCH FAMILY PROCESSES

As an emotional system, the church family has its own drama. It too confronts the perennial human needs for separateness and closeness in relationships. The church family has its "distancers" in the nonactive and the quitters. It has its share of "fusers" who consider the church family to be their property. Moreover, people act out their own unfinished agendas in other relationships with members of the congregation. Some are intent on haranguing others so that they don't have to change themselves. Some are forever cheating others of their birthright for their own special place in the family. Still others form a crankiness crowd, looking for external conditions to explain their own unhappiness. And what church family doesn't have a sunshine squad? Fearful of differences and differing, they brighten the family's life and distract it from threatening storm clouds.

Common to many church families is the unworked grief that surrounds the loss of an endeared pastor. Unable to let go and move ahead, some family members remain too emotionally attached to their Jacob or Esau. Regardless of the means of the pastor's exodus—replacement, retirement, forced resignation, or death—there is separation anxiety. Not resolved or managed, the anxiety turns into rejection of the new pastor, withdrawal from the family, or fervid attempts to fuse with the newly assigned or called pastor.

Other examples of the separateness and closeness forces at work in the church family come from my consultation experience. A church family that had grown from 100 to 600 members in five years went through a nine-month period without their pastor. He had been called to active duty during Desert Storm. During his absence a number of families from the original one hundred filled the vacuum and assumed control. When the pastor returned, he was stunned when this group approached him with a prepared letter of resignation, demanding his signature. Having lost their functioning positions with the influx of new members, they were ready to sell Joseph to settle their own anxiety. Eventually thirty-four members left. The pastor went to therapy, having absorbed too much of the anxiety of the dissidents.

Fresh out of seminary, Pastor Jack was eager to begin his public ministry in town. He arrived with his wife, two children, and a van with their belongings. The house designated for their use belonged to a prominent member of the congregation. But Jack and his wife found it in disrepair and unsuitable for their needs. He unloaded the furniture there but spent three days looking for another residence. He signed a contract for a lease with an option to buy and moved into it. The next six months were a nightmare for him and his family. Rumors began to circulate that he was an "an agent of Satan," that his nine-year-old son had been abused by his father, and that since he was from California he was either gay or liberal. More sensible members came to his defense. The prominent member and seven other families left. But the rumors persisted. As is so often the case, fusers, failing to achieve their ends, quit. They simply exchange one extreme for another.

For two years Pastor Mary had enjoyed success as the new associate pastor. Suddenly she sensed everything was coming apart. At a pastoral relation committee meeting, she was fiercely attacked by a member who was recently divorced. She was confused. The man who attacked her turned around and soothed her. His behavior continued—attack, then an offer of help or consolation. The senior pastor avoided the situation. She felt betrayed and isolated. I suggested that the male attacker's behavior was seductive, and the male senior pastor's evasive. She would need to define herself to both. "But how," she asked with desperation, "can a woman be assertive and not seem to be aggressive?"

To Mary's credit, she defined herself and stayed in touch—and managed her anxiety. It would have been easier to hide the problem and accede to the concern about how others might think of her. But she realized that what would have been easier for the moment would have been harder for the long run. By not beginning to define herself now, she would initiate a pattern of relating in which she acquiesced. She trusted in what is difficult. As the poet Rainer Maria Rilke reminds us, "That something is difficult must be one more reason for us to do it."

DIRECTING ENERGY

Anxiety directs higher energy to the reptilian brain. Intense anxiety can even turn the higher brains—the feeling and thinking capacities—to the service of the reptilian brain. Feelings become overpowering. Thinking is narrowly focused. The whole brain concentrates on self-defense alone. There is an inability to shut off the energy source to automatic processes. The higher brain no longer guides, directs, or modifies the crude instincts. The key question is how to transfer energy back to the House of Emotion and the Thinking Cap—to a sense of community and a sense of purpose; in other words, to compassion in concert with clarity. Loving one another does not mean merging, fusing, and staying stuck together. Those are symptomatic of anxiety, not a sign of respectful care. It is "mutual helplessness" (Rilke), without benefit and strength.

Chapter 4

Stability and Change

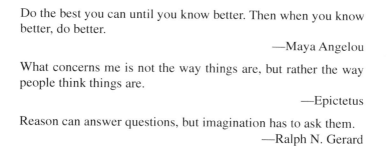

Do the best you can until you know better. Then when you know better, do better.

—Maya Angelou

What concerns me is not the way things are, but rather the way people think things are.

—Epictetus

Reason can answer questions, but imagination has to ask them.
—Ralph N. Gerard

THE CLOUD OF THREAT

In the fourteenth century the Great Mortality ravaged Europe. It spread swiftly and in a similar manner brought an end to life. More than a third of the population succumbed to the deadly blows of the plague. Ignorance of its cause magnified its horror. Some attributed the outbreak of the Black Death to the sign of the zodiac or to the presence of evil spirits. Among the masses the popular explanation was divine punishment for sin. Even though sanitary conditions were suspected as a possible source of the ravishing disease, they were not examined carefully.

Disease-carrying rats escaped detection, in part, because people needed sin-bearing scapegoats. In her book *A Distant Mirror*, historian Barbara Tuchman has noted that, despite the belief in divine wrath, "people in their misery still looked for a human agent upon whom to vent the hostility that could not be vented on God." The torment of the plague prompted many to assign malevolence to the Jews. They were charged with poisoning the wells to kill Christians and destroy Christendom. Thus, the Jews were subjected to persecution, expulsion, and the confiscation of their property.

Taking advantage of people's panic and their discontent with the church, hundreds of bands of "flagellants" went from town to town focusing people's hostility on the clergy and church authorities. With leather whips tipped with spikes, they scourged themselves until they bled. They contended that their self-torture would turn aside God's wrath, bringing an end to the interminable devastation of lives. In doing so, they took upon themselves the role of interceders with God, a role reserved exclusively for priests. When the church finally opposed their activity, the flagellants continued to excite people's frail emotions, redirecting their rage toward the Jews.

The Great Mortality left survivors with enormous uncertainty. They were at the mercy of their instinct to survive. They banded together, but their tight, frightened togetherness reduced their range of view. They could not see beyond their collective reactivity. To regain a sense of stability, they concentrated their anxiety on an object: fate, demons, Jews, priests.

Psycho-historian Robert Jay Lifton has identified the same emotional processes in the aftermath of the atomic explosions in Hiroshima and Nagasaki, Lifton discovered that survivors attributed the destruction and death to "cosmic retribution" for wrongdoing. Others, despite being victims rather than perpetrators, placed the responsibility for the catastrophe on themselves. They turned themselves into scapegoats. Panic also played its hand in rumors, such as the one that America would drop rotten pigs to hasten the decay of the land. Life was so suddenly and fundamentally altered that people expected only further and more bizarre consequences. Conspiracy is an old-time human explanation, especially in uncertain, anxious times.

Amanda Ripley's *The Unthinkable: Who Survives Disaster—and Why* discusses disasters such as flood, tsunami, fire, explosion, 9/11, and the role of fear, resilience, groupthink, panic, and heroism. There is no direct analysis of an epidemic (or our contemporary pandemic), yet her insights are valuable since she speaks about human responses to survival. She concludes her study by citing "three advantages" that those who perform effectively tend to have in crisis and recovery:

"They believe they can influence what happens to them"; "They find meaningful purpose in life's turmoil"; and "They are convinced they can learn from both good and bad experiences."

Ripley's study reminds me of Dr. Edwin Friedman's counsel that no matter how many or how strong stressors might be, the key factor is our response to them. In terms of today's COVID-19 threat, our responses (hand-washing, face masks, social distance, shelter in place) affect the way we handle the crisis. ("All it takes is the audacity to imagine that our behavior matters".)

The word "disaster" itself conveys insight into what we are dealing with in this strange time. In Greek "dis" can mean "ill" or "bad"; it can also be translated "away from" (distance). "Astrum" refers to a star. The ancients believed that the heavens gave direction to humans. Literally, a disaster is something unguided, without structure, bent beyond the normal, and catastrophic. Disaster runs wild, makes no sense, and renders life uncontrollable.

Heaven help us if our leaders can do no better than mimic the very disaster in combatting it. We need leaders who have the "three advantages" (agency, purpose, and the capacity to learn). Otherwise, their own untamed nature will cooperate with Nature's fury.

SHOCK WAVES

The black plague and the atomic holocaust had widespread and long-term outcomes. They were immense devastations. Still, shocks of lesser magnitude set off similar reactive forces. Systems need calm and coherence. They react swiftly to sudden shifts and marked differences. The survival instinct prevents them from being overwhelmed by unexpected or excessive change. When tested and challenged, systems move toward self-preservation, though their emotional reactivity will vary in intensity and duration.

It is not a sign of defectiveness or evil for a system to protect itself against what it cannot accommodate. Reactivity is in service of survival. But what is automatic is intended to be temporary, not permanent. If anxiety is reinforced and takes hold, it is locked into the system. After a while the system may even become loyal to its own reactivity.

When anxiety is high, resilience is low. Behaviors are extreme and rigid; thoughts are unclear and disjointed. Anxious people speak harsh words or cut themselves off from others through silence. To manage their threatening situation, people hurry to localize their anxiety. They blame and criticize. Yet it is one thing for a system to be shattered by shocking events and another to be shackled by its own reactive tremors. Once a system fortifies its stability by its reactivity, it cannot get what it needs most: time and distance, calm and objectivity, clarity and imagination. It is caught in its own automatic processes. But a relationship system does not live by reaction alone but by *every* resource at its disposal. Therefore, a system that maintains its stability by reactivity alone will not be stable in the long run. Continuous reactivity creates three processes that prevent the system from being resourceful and flexible—a *shrinking of perspective*, *a tightening of the circle*, and a *shifting of the burden*. Consequently, it is not apt to repair itself, plan for the future, or find a new direction.

A NARROW PERSPECTIVE

When we as individuals are anxious, we cannot distance ourselves enough from the threat to be objective and even-minded. For instance, if we are "at odds" with someone, chances are we will not "play even."

Stories are shaded; information is withheld. Complaints are vague. The faults of others are exaggerated. When emotionality sweeps over the Thinking Cap, our view is blunted. We see through a dark glass. Often we have to appeal to a third party for a more thoughtful, impartial judgment than we ourselves can render.

Anxious systems also fail to get a clear view of things. Embedded in their dread, they lose a sense of proportion. They have little awareness of what is happening and how it is being mutually maintained. Emotionality cramps the broader view.

Reading the Hebrew Scriptures, we discover many cases of distorted perceptions in anxious circumstances. With their perspective skewed, the Israelites seek safety in structures. For the sake of stability, they build the golden calf and devise plans for the Tower of Babel. Then, on the borders of Canaan, the spies return from the unknown land and report excitely, "The people over there are GIANTS!" Terrified, the spies enlarge the size of these foreigners. Later we find the "comforters" of Job who, anxious about life's randomness, offer Job one-sided explanations for his major losses. And Hezekiah, who though he received a fifteen-year divine guarantee of stability, hedges the promise by making deals with foreign foes.

Throughout these events God sends prophets to open the people's eyes and to expand their horizon. As we know, though, true prophets are without honor in their own anxious country. Many of God's messengers are ignored, mocked, or annihilated. But the false prophets who cry, "Peace, peace," and heal the wounds of the people lightly are too often welcomed. They promise stability but invite no reflection. False prophets offer simple, immediate relief. They don't challenge people to change their limited points of view.

THE TIGHT CIRCLE

Anxiety blinds us. We have difficulty perceiving that in which we are emotionally entangled. We see the trees but not the forest, the part but not the whole. Anxiety also blinds us. We have trouble separating ourselves from the pressure of togetherness. Most of us are afraid of losing one another's support. As television writer Norman Lear reminded us, being a self isn't such a great thing because it doesn't seem to be what anyone else wants. And at anxious periods, the forces for sameness and like-mindedness are even greater.

In the epilogue to the book *The Devils of Loudon*, Aldous Huxley presents a commentary on anxious systems. The book recites the history of mass hysteria in the Ursuline convent in the town of Loudon. The nuns, believing they are possessed, accuse a priest of bewitching them. Eventually he is executed. Huxley sees the story as more than a piece of history in the village of Loudon. It is a parable of an anxious system: people escaping consciousness and searching for bogus stability. In a healthy, purposeful community, Huxley says, men and women have a certain capacity for thought and discrimination. Under the spell of automatic processes, the same individuals behave as if they possess neither good sense nor judgment.

Huxley discusses "herd-poison" as a way to deliver a man or woman from awareness, choice, and responsibility. In their place there is "only a strong vague sense of togetherness, a shared excitement, a collective alienation." Huxley claims that excited masses fall into mindlessness. They drug themselves on their own frenzy. Challenging the church, Huxley remarks:

"Where two or three are gathered together in my name, there I am in the midst of them." In the midst of two or three hundred, the divine presence becomes more problematical. And when the numbers run into the thousands, the likelihood of God being there, in the consciousness of each individual, declines almost to the vanishing point. For such is the nature of an excited crowd (and every crowd is automatically self-excited) that, where two or three thousand are gathered together, there is an absence not merely of deity, but even of common humanity. (*The Devils of Loudon*, p. 317)

Intoxicated by its own excited togetherness, the crowd cannot focus outside itself. In a stupor, God is hardly the focal point.

"Crowd delirium" is fed by both emotional extremes—ecstasy and anxiety. Both numb the thinking processes. Whether it is ecstasy or anxiety that is stupefying the system, the same result occurs, "an absence not merely of deity, but even of common humanity."

People can be emotionally connected to one another not only by shared excitement but also by mutual hostility. Herd-poison comes in doses of both frenzy and fury. As long as people function in reciprocally reactive ways, there is little emotional separation between them. Even though they may withdraw physically from one another or stand at opposite ideological poles, they will nonetheless be emotionally linked by their reinforcing reactivity to one another. When people cannot stay out of each other's emotional orbit, they are powerfully connected. Thus the circle is tightened just as much by furious belligerence as spontaneous uproar.

THE SHIFTED BURDEN

Relationship systems are always, to some degree, unstable. Sharp tension makes the instability transparent. Inevitably, the most anxious people in the system bind their anxiety by shifting to pain killers or placing the pain elsewhere. They shift their own burden elsewhere. To reduce the strain, they draw in someone or something else. In my consulting work with anxious church families, I have kept track of the people who were pinning their hurt or emptiness outside of themselves. About 5 percent of them were chronically anxious. No matter what "the bone of contention" may have been, these individuals would have reacted. The greater number, however, was acutely anxious. They had experienced traumatization within the last few years. Unable to manage their anxiety, they played it out on the congregational stage, shifting their anxiety to an issue or a person. The list below identifies and enumerates the kinds of emotionally laden changes that had preceded their outbursts. The list is compiled from approximately 200 people.

Disruptions

(32)	loss of a job
(19)	economic woes
(11)	business upheaval
(7)	bankruptcy
(20)	grief or anger related to former pastor
(12)	transferred membership after experiencing discord in previous congregation
(15)	major life crises
(14)	alcoholism
(26)	marital strife
(19)	unhappiness of a spouse
(17)	divorce
(9)	death of a spouse
(12)	serious accidents (family member involved)
(12)	pregnant or sexually active teenager
(10)	child leaves home
(13)	death of a child
(8)	child with social adjustment, substance abuse, or academic difficulties
(14)	tension in extended family
(17)	illness or death of a parent
(11)	relocation of family

It is important to note that not all individuals undergoing such events become reactive and find a target for their discomfort. But the listing is instructive. It bears out the axiom that anxiety not resolved in one relationship will be focused in another relationship.

TRIANGLES

The most common way to bind anxiety is through the emotional process of triangling. Pastoral counselor David Augsburger has wryly stated, "It takes three to *tangle*." When A is at odds with B, the most anxious of the pair introduces C (third party) to reduce anxiety between A and B. For example, God confronts Adam about his disobedience. Anxious, Adam shifts the burden to Eve. When she encounters God, Eve blames the snake. (See Diagram 4.1.)

The wilderness temptations of Jesus are set in the same triangular process. The Tempter attempts to put God in the C position: on the outside. If only Jesus would command the stones, hurl himself from the pinnacle, or bow to the tempter, then all the power and kingdoms would be his. But Jesus "de-triangulates" himself. He stays focused on and committed to the word of God.

Burden shifting is three-sided. It involves three people, or two people and a mood, or two people and a substance. When someone shifts the burden, another person or thing will be placed in the outside position. Gossip, for instance, is a triangle with two people on the inside and a third on the outside. Yet as Friedman warns, "In the concept of an emotional triangle, what Peter says to you about his relationship with Paul has to do with his relationship with you." Or think about an angry brother who remarks to his younger sister, "Now do you think God would approve of what you're doing?" She moves her anxiety to her brother and divine authority. Or a husband blurts out to his wife, "Why can't you be like other wives?" The husband's anxiety is relocated from his wife and himself to his wife and other wives.

In a church family you might find these types of triangles. Fearful of expressing his feelings directly, an irate church member says, "Pastor,

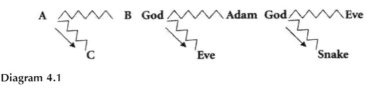

Diagram 4.1

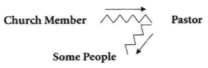

Diagram 4.2

some people are saying . . ." Using others to cloak his feelings, the member shifts the burden to the pastor and the vague "some people." (See Diagram 4.2.)

A pastor manipulates a member of the governing board to sway the rest of the board toward favoring the pastor's position. The single board member is set up to do the pastor's bidding with the other board members. (See Diagram 4.3.)

A member who has undergone a major life crisis (such as those listed previously) suddenly becomes critical of the pastor. Although anxiety lies within other relationships, the pastor is drawn into the picture. (See Diagram 4.4.)

The person who ends up with anxiety (the third party, C position) is called the "burden bearer" or "scapegoat" or "identified patient." Though this may not be too comforting for clergy and key lay leaders, they are potentially a member of every triangle of every family in the congregation.

In some cases I have also found an "identified problem." Whenever a certain church family is anxious, it focuses its anxiety on the same spot—"the budget," or "the bishop," or "the past," or "the unfriendliness." Many times the identified problem is the pastoral office. In fact, some church families have a history of shifting their burden to the pastor. The source of the burden may not have much to do with the pastor. Yet these systems focus their anxiety on that position. It is automatic. It is their norm for regaining stability.

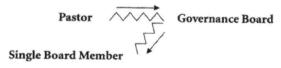

Diagram 4.3

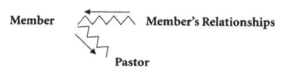

Diagram 4.4

PRIME TARGETS

The individuals in any system who are most likely to be triangulated are those who are in the responsible or vulnerable position. The children, for example, who are apt to be the focus of their parents' anxiety are the oldest and youngest (often the most responsible and vulnerable). In larger systems we see the same process. I consulted with a seminary faculty and staff entrenched in a conflict. To the first session, I brought three grocery bags full of grapefruits, oranges, and lemons. I assigned weight to each type of fruit—a grapefruit equaled twenty-five pounds of anxiety; an orange, ten; and a lemon, five. I asked the dean of students to distribute the citrus fruit according to whom he thought had the most to the least anxiety. Everyone was given the chance to exchange the fruit with others if they thought they had too much or too little of the burden. When finished, the individuals who had all the grapefruits and most of the oranges were the dean of the seminary and the provost (most responsible) and the four untenured professors (most vulnerable). Working with an anxious church staff of nine people, I repeated the procedure. Again, the majority of grapefruits and oranges rested in the hands of the senior pastor and the two staff members whose job descriptions were changing most significantly.

I want to mention a situation which merits special attention. If the pastor occupies both positions, being the most responsible and the most vulnerable at the same time, the pastor may be unfairly, if not mercilessly, attacked. I have seen three clergy whose children had been killed, two whose spouses died of cancer, and four who suffered other losses become the center of careless and irrational criticism. Conventional wisdom would lead us to believe that such circumstances would bring an abundance of compassion and tolerance. What happened, I believe, is that some anxious members needed the pastor to function at the same level as before the losses. But the clergy were hurting and grieving. Their normal functioning was impaired. Nonetheless, the anxious members needed their pastor to be strong, energetic, approachable, and the like. Needing security, the anxious forces reacted and focused negatively upon the pastor. The pastor in crisis jars the stability of the whole system. And some will demand a return to stability, even if it means forcing the pastor to be "the old self" again through distasteful means. Many of the attackers had no awareness of what they were doing. Overfocused on this pastor, they had no focus on self. They could not recognize how anxious they were because the pastor was in crisis.

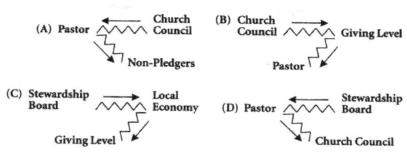

Diagram 4.5

THE TRIANGULAR WEB

Because no emotional system stays calm, triangles always develop to bind anxiety. The less flexible the system, the more the burden is shifted to the same person, the same functioning position, or the same location. Moreover, triangles oppose change. They maintain reactivity. Without resilience, therefore, the system stays tied up in its own emotional knots. The triangles interlock. Like "the buck," anxiety is passed around. Instead of recognizing how anxiety is being mutually reinforced, the system searches for a cause or a culprit. Individuals shift the burden from here to there and back to here. They become focused on weaknesses, diagnosis, and troublemakers. The overall relationship patterns are lost to awareness.

A church family suffering financial problems can be used to illustrate the triangular web. See Diagram 4.5 for a list of some possible parts of the problem.

CHURCH COUNCIL

Consider just a few examples of how these parts can be interlocked in triangles. In triangle A, the pastor and church council confront the financial problem by focusing on members who do not pledge, noting that nonpledgers give less than pledgers. Triangle B reveals the church council's anxiety about the general giving level of the whole system and shifts the burden to the pastor because of lack of leadership in this area. Meanwhile the stewardship board realizes that the local economy is depressed and attributes the decline in giving level to the recession (C). In yet another triangle (D) the pastor and the stewardship board deal with their anxiety by pinning it on the church council for lack of planning and vision.

As long as anxiety is shifted and interlocked, the system will remain captive to its own emotional processes. Too intent on binding its anxiety, the system is not able to use it as a means for change and adaptation. The system is not interested in learning from its pain. It merely wants to escape. "Scared stiff," the system cannot be resourceful and flexible. But shifting the burden does not lift the burden; it merely relocates it. Not until the emotional process is seen and interrupted will substantive changes occur. In other words, thinking must regulate automatic processes. The defining of self must replace the defining of others.

REDEFINING

A system needs change as well as stability. Living things grow and develop. They are not static. There is a time for sameness, and a time for transformation . . . a time to survive, and a time to risk . . . a time for reaction, and a time for reflection . . . a time to be stable, and a time to be resilient. One of the most effective ways to introduce change is to redefine the problem—to see the whole pattern of interaction. Redefining affects the Thinking Cap. It intervenes into narrow viewpoints, tightened circles, and shifted burdens.

Let me illustrate what happened at First Church when it redefined its problem. A conflict had been brewing for six months, in the latter half of the new pastor's second year. Grumbling and discontent strained many relationships. The pastor was baffled. He indicated that he had never in his twenty years as a parish pastor experienced anything like the present tension. Many people also expressed disbelief at the pettiness and meanness of the discord.

I contracted to work with twenty leaders of First Church. At one point in the process, I divided them into five groups. After asking each group to cite three problems, I gave them the assignment to redefine the problem *without* focusing solely on a person or issue as presented in the original problem. Some of their responses are noted in table 4.1.

Both the pastor and the leaders began to see their problems as *a whole*, as a matter of *mutual influence*. After they redefined their problem, they had a whole new perspective—and they were thinking *systemically*.

Table 4.1

Presenting Problem	Redefined Problem
The pastor isn't effective. He's not feeding us spiritually.	The pastor's style of ministry and our expectations do not match well. We have had trouble adjusting to a new pastor. We want the pastor to be like our former pastor.
The pastor is too greedy. He never stops talking about money.	We have been conservative in granting pay raises. We have no salary policy or standard. We are used to a pastor who accepted minimal salary increases.
The chemistry is bad. It's unfortunate. The pastor is a nice person but doesn't fit here. The bishop should have known better than to give us this man's name for consideration.	We have discovered that we are accustomed to a quiet, scholarly type of pastor. Our current pastor's approach is more aggressive and down-to-earth. We have some resistance to the challenges our pastor puts before us. The bishop wanted to shake us loose from our complacency and stir up our potential.
The pastor sets one group against another. He's determined to divide and conquer.	The pastor is bringing about change. Some of us like it; some of us don't. Before he came we asked the pastor to "get us going." But we never stated clearly what we really wanted. A difference of opinion existed among us about change (what, how, and when) even before the pastor arrived.

With anxiety slackening, they were ready to proceed to the next step toward change. It was yet another kind of definition: self-definition. Instead of defining themselves against one another, they resolved to define themselves *to* one another. As long as there is blaming, it is nearly impossible to institute change. Blaming is a sign that people are stuck in their instinctive nature. The blame game resembles an ancient religious practice called "divination"—locating the source of evil (which is believed to be outside of oneself) and eliminating it. Though churches unfortunately use it, the practice has no biblical sanction.

To continue the change process, I introduced the leaders to a set of ten questions designed to move them toward reflection. Note the list below and observe how the questions are directed toward resources not damages, strength not weakness, imagination not reaction, and challenge not answers. Haranguing people will hardly change them. It may force accommodation, but that is not the same as transformation.

1. What would it look like if you were happy, satisfied?
2. What is weakening your resources and strength?
3. Write a sentence to describe your problem. Then redefine your problem in another sentence without reference to a *single* issue or person.
4. Who are the most motivated people in the congregation?
5. Where's your plan? What's your vision?
6. What would it take to have a pastor stay here ten years, twenty years?
7. What would be your own signs of a healthy congregation?
8. Can you imagine this congregation in five years being alive, thriving, etc.? How would you know it happened?
9. How would you be willing to invest yourself in the process of creating the image you defined above?
10. How do you understand what is happening here theologically or biblically?

Finally I worked with the leaders to make *specific* changes. Vagueness is on the side of the status quo. Generalities favor homeostasis. Change must be defined, and it must come from people who are capable of defining themselves, who know where they want to go and what they want to accomplish.

Without the process I introduced, First Church may have continued to flounder, perhaps deepen its "stuckness". I don't want to leave the impression that the process worked magic. Its effectiveness rested with the *maturity* of the leaders who were *motivated* to change.

Chapter 5

Clarity and Compassion

My husband said to me, "Honey, you worry too much about people!" I said, 'I don't worry, I care!'

—Pearl Bailey

Difficult as it is really to listen to someone in affliction, it is just as difficult for him to know that compassion is listening to him.

—Simone Weil

We are used to thinking of compassion as an emotional state, based on our concern for one another. But it is also grounded in a level of awareness.

—Peter Senge

THE HEAD AND THE HEART

The word "church" has its origin in the word *kyrike*. It means "belonging to the Lord." The church is a people drawn together in the resurrected Christ. More than thirty times, the apostle Paul uses the metaphor of "the body of Christ," with Christ as "the head" and the people as "the body," to illustrate their connectedness. Like the numerous, specialized organs of the human body, the people who compose the body of Christ are many and their functions are different. Our bodies would not be fully functioning entities if their parts were all "ears" or all "eyes." They require diversity. In fact, it is the magnificent diversity of cells in our bodies that enables us to function at a high level. This is as true for a body of people as it is for a body of an individual person. When a group is diverse, it is more resourceful, having many ideas, gifts, and functions at work. What is common to the many parts is the head. The head draws the parts together, and the parts draw their life from the head. In the church there is the *same Lord* who, obviously, as its head, enjoys variety.

The church is a gathering of dissimilar parts. It is not necessary that the parts be identical to one another. It is necessary that they be identified with one another. Those who have the same Lord are to have the *same care* for one another. Belonging to the Lord through faith is inseparable from belonging to the parts through care. The church, striking in its diversity, is most effective in its working together for mutual benefit. When care is applied unevenly or inconsistently, mutuality is undermined. Life together is unbalanced.

I want, however, to address another weakening of mutuality. We are less familiar with its distorting effect. We confuse care with emotionality. It's as if in caring there is no connection between the Thinking Cap and the House of Emotion. Misunderstood as sentiment alone, care is stripped of the power of thoughtfulness. It has energy but no boundary; it has speed but no direction. When we do not use our thinking capacities, we turn care into something soft or melodramatic. We equate it with being meekly pleasant and obliging or being hypersensitive and excessively concerned. Indeed the heart has its reasons which the head cannot know, but conversely the head has its reasons which the heart cannot see. The head gives to the heart a sense of responsibility, proportion, and discrimination.

BLIND SPACE

"Love is blind," we say. Even the ancient Romans acknowledged the whimsical nature of romantic love in the creation of Cupid who would not allow his lover to see him. Henry Mencken jibed about lovers being in a condition of "perceptual anaesthesia." Wrapped up in each other's entrancing glow, what chance is there that two people can stand back sufficiently to see each other distinctively? I have often joked about the ineffectiveness of premarital counseling, adding, "What can you tell two psychotics?" Caught in sweet oblivion, they cannot access the power of discernment. They mistake the ideal for the real. Romantic love is the tie that binds—and blinds. No doubt, it makes a contribution to mutuality. But it is not mutuality itself. Mutuality is connectedness, not stickiness. "Gooey" interaction is emotional fusion. People lose their "self" in emotional knots. In mutuality each "self" is preserved and respected even while connection is made. There are spaces in their relationship. "We often think that when we have completed our study of one," Sir Arthur Eddington observes, "we know all about two, because 'two is one and one.' We forget that we have still to make a study of 'and.'" So there is a difference between the relationship of Bob and Betty and Bobandbetty. Bob and Betty have separateness *in* their relationship. Bobandbetty functions as a single entity. They are stuck together. Instead of joining together like Bob and Betty, they gel.

Romance is sticky. Confused as over-sensitivity or mellowness, care produces the same sticky results. There is little emotional separateness between people; there is a pull toward sameness. People suspend or sacrifice their own beliefs, values, or goals in order to keep life smooth and equal. They exchange integrity for harmony. "Soft care" is so devilish because it has desirable ends: the dulling of sharp edges and upsetting contrasts. But it achieves a spurious peace. We believe we can only be close if we are the same or tucked tightly together. Differences must be denied or neglected.

What we often don't realize is that sentimental care is anxiety driven. It comes from a sense of helplessness rather than helpfulness. Our glossy good-will, "peace-agree" position, and overprotective involvement with others is an expression of our own low toleration of pain. We cannot stand the tension and conflict that erupts when differences and contrasts appear. Like the ecstasy of romance, anxiety closes the space between people. Ecstasy and anxiety abhor spaces. They liquidate boundaries and limits; they stifle self-definition.

ANXIETY BINDS

Sentimentalists cannot distinguish their anxiety from their empathy. They confuse their own need to be less anxious in the face of pain with true regard for another. Thus they rescue others. They take over the life of helpless souls. Sometimes they appease others and give up their own souls. Sentimentalists cannot balance sensitivity with awareness.

Being an emotional system, the church family is tempted to submerge its anxiety in a sentimental swamp, In fact, Anne Wilson Schaef, a noted writer on addictions, has stated that "one of the greatest encouragers of niceness is the church." If she is right, the community chartered for mutuality has become a group of people fastened together by lightweight sentiment. Even more, it is a community unaware that below its niceness lies anxiety. It is a community in dread of its own diversity and often forgetful of its true unity—*kyrike*.

Matching Schaef's observation is an indictment Friedman has repeatedly made in his lectures:

> Actually religious institutions are the worst offenders at encouraging immaturity and irresponsibility. In church after church, some member is passively-aggressively holding the whole system hostage, and no one wants to fire him or force her to leave because it wouldn't be "the Christian thing to do." It has nothing to do with Christianity. Synagogues also tolerate abusers because it wouldn't be the Christian thing to do.

Friedman contends that *reactors* command many church families. He characterizes the reactors as the least mature, least motivated, least self-regulating, but most recalcitrant people. It is one thing to lament their "emotional leaking," but there is always a second part to the equation. There are *accomplices*. Relationships are "co-causal." Others permit and tolerate the taking of hostages; worse yet, they do it "in the name of love." A friend of mine calls this mode of operation "sloppy agape." Certainly we are to turn the other cheek, to walk the second mile, and to forgive our offenders seven times seventy. But we are encouraged to do "the Christian thing" to advance mutuality, not to abolish it. Our goal is to restore relationships, not to reinforce sulking, irritable, stubborn, even brutish behaviors. There is a world of difference between extending the hand of generosity and enabling reactive processes. Reactors have the greatest difficulty in controlling their anxiety. They let it "fly." Moreover, reactors thrive when others are passive or permissive toward their reactivity. Thus the anxious reactivity of the hostage taker is maintained by the sentimentality of the "nice" people.

Some people, of course, play hardball with the hostage takers. They explode with counterattacks. But both hostility and docility are reactive positions and not *defined* positions. Either way, they feed the crankiness. It is simple to recognize animosity as a hindrance to mutuality.

We fight fire with fire. Heat and smoke increase. The consequences of soft care are not as apparent. The reactors are bought off and pacified. Tempers cool off and faces lighten. The symptoms disappear. From the look of things, calm is reestablished. But how long will the truce last when one party goes home with all the marbles? How many more pay-offs will be required? And how many other petulant forces will emerge for their peace dividend?

TOLERATION OF PAIN

Each person has a comfort zone with pain: what they can bear and tolerate. Beyond that point, anxiety takes siege. Reactors have a low threshold for pain. They are automatically geared and careless about boundaries. They cannot maintain their own boundaries through self-definition; they are unable to respect the boundaries of others. Anxious, they are preoccupied with self-preservation. When others make adjustments in their functioning to relieve the reactors' distress, they reinforce the reactors' low toleration of pain. Sentimental care is one of those adjustments. It is also indicative of a low threshold for tolerating pain in others.

Diagram 5.1 illustrates the functioning positions we might take when the two comfort zones meet.

Quadrant A indicates toleration of pain in self but low toleration of pain in others (a scenario for rescuers who will suffer "compassion fatigue"). *Quadrant B* shows toleration of pain in self and others (a case of taking responsibility for self and being able to challenge others to do the same for themselves). *Quadrant C* displays low toleration of pain in self and others (a situation in which one acts helpless and commiserates with other helpless people: "Misery loves company"). *Quadrant D* depicts toleration of pain in others but low toleration in self (a circumstance in which one's own pain is always worse than anyone else's: "Woe is me").

There are many other possibilities. For instance, person A (low toleration of pain in self) connects with person B (low toleration of pain in others). The result is the classic dependent/co-dependent relationship. Another complementary relationship consists of the super-complainer and the hypersensitive pleaser. The powerless victim and the overzealous sentimentalist are also a pair of magnets. Then, too, there is person

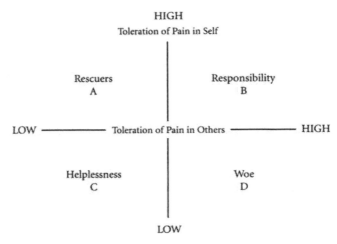

Diagram 5.1

C (high toleration of pain in others) relating with person D (low toleration of pain in self). Person D will likely manipulate person C to take care of her. Person C, if she is mature, will challenge person D to focus on her own coping capacities.

THE ANXIETY TRAP

Relationship systems develop their own comfort zones. During intense or protracted periods of emotional pain, they are apt to gravitate toward Quadrant C, or lower toleration. Painless, swift cures are often pursued. The comforters emerge using the medication of good cheer to quell the system's fever. The blamers arise, too. They pin their path on a culprit. Unfortunately they do not see themselves or the group as a whole as part of the emotional processes that are occurring.

Anxiety is an emotional pain. It is a given in relationship systems. The key is always how it is processed and managed. The more the system drifts toward Quadrant C, the less able it is to deal with anxiety responsibly. Instead it becomes reactive. Its attempts to minimize, anesthetize, or relocate anxiety in others are all signals of anxiety. When any of this happens, anxiety is managing the system. To the detriment of everyone, there is no discrimination response or clarity.

With imagination limited, the range of response is narrow. Automatic processes prevail. But as long as a relationship system remains in a self-preservation mode, it cannot *learn* from its crisis.

HEALTH IS A RESPONSE

We are not powerless. We are not as bound by our instincts as we appear to be. Reaction is a front line of defense. It is structured into life to be immediate. It is first but not necessarily foremost. We have other managing resources. Medical missionary Paul Brand has said that the ultimate design of pain is to be *directional*, whether it is physical, emotional, or spiritual pain. "It hurts not in order to cause discomfort," Brand elaborates, "but to demand a change in response to danger." Hypersensitivity serves as a "quick adaptation." But following hyper-sensitivity, the physical body, for example, "relies on the second level of response: distribution of stress." Like a healthy body, a healthy relationship system does not overfocus its anxiety on one spot or look for one simple solution. Rather it calls for a larger and more directed response. Hence if we sprain our left ankle, we shift our weight to our right leg and limp. If we develop a tender spot on our palm through pressure or friction, we lighten our grip or use our other hand. However, when we have a low toleration of pain in self and others, we do not learn to disperse pain or to make a change in our response. We keep living in the same hurting spot. We try to remedy anxiety with anxiety, but we only reinforce our powerlessness. Potentially, however, we have a pool of resources, a many-splendored repertoire of responses and a wealth of recuperative powers. We need not be merely instinctive in dealing with pain. "We are not committed or bound by our genes," Lewis Thomas, former president of the Sloan Kettering Center in New York City, notes, "to stick to one activity forever, like the wasps."

Notice how healing is built into life itself. Tired, we relax and sleep. Awakened, we begin afresh. Wounds heal. Broken bones knit together. Each day our circulatory system regenerates our blood. Every seven years our cellular system replaces itself. Our psyche, too, responds to loss and hurt with self-renewing mechanisms that redistribute emotional pain. Not only within us but also around us, there are forces of regeneration: someone's touch, a significant person's presence, a con-soler's words.

Relationship systems can be renewed and made whole. But the wholeness emerges only when we go beyond our initial hypersensitivity and make use of our second level of response, responding discriminately, consciously, and objectively. Without such clarity we have little sense of direction. We neither manage our own response nor stimulate the response of others.

NAMING THE DEMONS

Upon seeing the people helpless and harassed, Jesus *took compassion* on them. And he began to *teach* them. His compassion did not issue from a low comfort zone with pain. He did not over-function; he did not rescue them. He *taught* them. He raised their thinking capacities. He cared by staying connected (compassion) and staying defined (teaching). From the accounts of the Gospels, we might assume that he made clear statements to them: "Truly, I say." (definition, information). He asked questions to stimulate the people's responses and to activate their power of discrimination. "Who do you say I am?" (Mark 9:20). "What do you want me to do for you?" (Luke 18:41). "Can you drink the cup of suffering I must drink?" (Mark 10:38). "Do you love me?" (John 21:16). To stir up people's imagination, Jesus told stories. A statement attributed to Albert Einstein advises telling stories and more stories to increase the thinking capacity.

The story in Mark 5:1–20 gives us a closer look at how Jesus cared by combining compassion with clarity. I have selected this story of the Gerasene demoniac because everyone reacts. The demons react, the pigs react, the men watching the pigs react, the townspeople react, and the man who had been possessed reacts.

A man possessed by demons dwells among the tombs. Exiled from others and chained to protect himself from himself, he breaks each new set of fetters. Day and night, he cries aloud among the hillsides and cuts himself with stone. Calmly in the face of the pain's demented destructiveness, Jesus asks the voices to name themselves. They cry out that they are named "Legion," meaning many. But then comes an incredibly strange reaction from the possessed man: "Do not torment me!" We would have expected, "Free me. Let me loose from this world of horror!" But we have to remember how wedded we become even to our chains. Without them we will be held responsible for our actions.

The demons are exorcised and fill the pigs that stampede to their death. The herders react. Shocked, they run into town to report the events to the people there. A horde comes out of town, jostled by curiosity and anxiety. They react: "Get out!" A man is now in his right mind and about to be restored to his community, and they ask the healer to leave. Weren't the events, though, asking them to rethink reality and familiar ideas, even to ask whether or not their life was their own?

Finally the man who is made whole reacts. He begs to go with Jesus. The man could now discover what real life is about, and yet he wants to follow the teacher who helped him. Quietly, looking at the man, Jesus breaks his silence: "Go to your own folk and tell them what the Lord in his mercy has done for you." No dependency. No freak show. No living proof of Jesus's power. None of that. Rather, there is true compassion. "Be free. Define yourself and stay in touch with your own folk." In the presence of all the clamorous anxiety, Jesus alone has the capacity to respond. Not deterred by the reactivity engulfing him. Jesus challenges the man who is healed to be responsive.

PURPOSE BONDING

Anxious church families become locked in emotional reactivity. This is quite evident when they fight openly and angrily—what I call "short fuse" fusion. Less obvious is another kind of emotional binding. Rather than facing off against each other, people make trade-offs. The reactive herdsmen and townspeople are treated with "kid gloves" or the "soft shoe." Nevertheless, sentimentalism is as reactive as pugilism. Many churches like to fight emotional fires with sprinkling cans. Preferring "homey togetherness," they are cautious to avoid, as much as possible, hard feelings or hurt feelings. Sentimentalists, having low toleration of pain, cannot see that they are mistaking appeasing for loving. Further, they cannot recognize that their empathy is related more to their own need to be relieved of their anxiety in the presence of pain than to genuine care for the hurting.

Sentimentalists seldom realize that reactors have "holes in their buckets." They are poor containers. No matter how much ground you give, how many peace proposals you offer, or what sound reasons you present, it is to no advantage. What is given in care is not received or appreciated. It leaks out as quickly as water from a bucket with holes.

More will be expected. Meanwhile the reactors are not held responsible for their actions and are shielded from challenge. Consequently they continue to function so that others will take care of them, comfort them, and surrender to their emotional bargaining. In turn, sentimentalists, functioning in anxious feedback positions, give and give, sacrificing their own integrity and sustaining the reactivity of the anxious.

There is no way that we could construe such an arrangement as mutuality. It is reciprocal but not beneficial to either side. Mutuality is reciprocal but always to the gain of the whole. For the whole to gain, care must combine compassion and clarity. The latter is what is missing in intense emotional binding. We know how relatively easy it is to discern problems in another person objectively, if we are not too close to them. How much more troublesome it is to see our own problems and those of the people closest to us. And how much more difficult it is for us, like the herders and the villagers, to handle the surprising and new when we are adjusted to the old. We care more, not less, when people are closer and events are more familiar to us. Thus there will be greater emotional energy, whether it is anger, fear, pity, or compassion. But we lose perspective and proportion. "Get out of our country" (cut off), or "Let me go with you" (fusion). We have less power to discriminate when we are emotionally entangled.

The capacity to differentiate is the capacity to be *clear* about boundaries, responsibilities, and goals. Differentiation marks the outlines of a person. It separates self from others. It specifies a difference—I. Differentiation also marks the parameters of the other person. It separates others from self. Differentiation supports the other person's "I" position. Differentiation is the ability to be aware of one's self and the other's self at the same time. It means that we can be compassionate with other people without being engulfed or determined by them. It means we can be clear about our response to others without being responsible for them. None of this is easy: It is even harder when emotionality is intense.

Friedman uses the biblical story of the golden calf to distinguish between the undifferentiated sentimentalist and the differentiated caregiver. Aaron is too sensitive to people's pain. He wants only to relieve their incessant, nagging complaints. But Moses is on a quest for truth. He will not heal the people's pain with some narcotic or magic. "The reason, by the way," Friedman mentions, "that Moses has a higher threshold for his people's pain than Aaron is because Moses has vision."

Without clarity people perish in their emotional intensity. They are not challenged sufficiently to raise their threshold for pain and thereby to respond to life instead of reacting against it. They stay mired in their automatic behaviors. They cannot see that they have come together for something more than self-preservation; they forget that they form a whole to respond to something larger than themselves. Intense emotional binding sweeps aside the recognition and awareness that the church family bonds together for purposes that the reptilian brain cannot know.

Part II

THE CONGREGATION AS
AN EMOTIONAL SYSTEM

Chapter 6

Do Not Go Gently into
That Glob of Glue

Once the realization is accepted
That even between the closest human beings
Infinite distances continue to exist
A wonderful living side by side can grow up
If they succeed in loving the distance between them
Which makes it possible for each to see the other
Whole and against a wide sky.

—Rainer Maria Rilke

No need to hurry. No need to sparkle. No need to be anybody but oneself.

—Virginia Woolf

A "differentiated self" is one who can maintain emotional objectivity, while in the midst of an emotional system in turmoil, yet at the same time actively relate to key people in the system.

—Murray Bowen

EMOTIONAL PROCESSES

Imagine a family of four people. They have refurbished their house and have built an addition onto it. Within a year of completion, the father of the family loses his job when his small company merges with a larger one. He is unemployed for nine months and eventually accepts a new position that pays less than his previous job. During the same period

71

of time, his son is injured in an auto accident and recovers slowly. His mother consumes all of her vacation time and accumulated sick leave to attend to his recovery. Anxiety permeates their family life.

Now imagine a church family of 400. They repair the existing church structure and construct a new educational unit. Unexpectedly, a manufacturing plant in town closes, throwing the town's economy into a tailspin. In turn, the church family's financial resources are affected adversely. At the same time one of the part-time staff suffers a serious illness and takes an extended leave of absence. Just like the family of four, the church family of 400 is riddled with anxiety.

Certainly, the family's anxiety will be more intense and concentrated than the congregation's. In the church family, anxiety will be more dispersed, affecting some people more than others. Nonetheless, both the nuclear family and the church family are relationship systems subject to the same emotional processes.

A second scenario: Imagine a pastor in his mid-forties who has recently buried his mother. His sixteen-year-old daughter breaks off a relationship with a young man the family likes and develops a fondness for a high school dropout five years her senior. A change of leadership takes place in the congregation and a number of key members are transferred. The pastor is anxious. He manages it by pasting on his clergy smile and donning his clergy robe of self-sufficiency. He functions like a hospital patient who is cheerful and cooperative to take care of his caregivers. He makes few requests and asks fewer questions. He gives the appearance of well-being so as not to upset the system. He de-selfs to protect the self.

Now imagine a key figure in the church's structure. She and her husband are living together physically but not happily. She has secured a loan to keep her small business operating, yet she knows her lender will not extend any additional credit. Her younger brother is about to stand trial on charges of drunken driving. To make matters worse, her father badgers her to help her brother with the cost of his legal defense. She's anxious. She manages it by pulling back, being noncommunicative and sullen. Her responsibilities with the church suffer. Pressured for action, she makes excuses and avoids contact with members. She functions like a student who never completes her homework, becomes truant, and withdraws from normal school activities. She distances to preserve the self.

The above examples are real-life situations about emotional functioning. They happen with more frequency than is realized. Major shifts occur in the lives of people, setting off emotional processes and testing their managing and coping capacities. "The outcome of interactions with the environment," the noted stress theorist Hans Selye remarks, "depends just as much upon our reaction to the stressors as upon the nature of the stress itself." In the next three chapters, we will look at the congregation as an emotional system. We will examine the emotional processes and response/reaction capacities in four church families. We begin with a situation in which we'll see the emotional process of fusion, interlocking triangles, and anxious leadership.

THE SEEN AND THE NOT SEEN

A quick glance at Transfiguration Church would evoke immediate awe. The church would be the envy of the laity and the desire of the clergy. Its membership exceeds 2,000 and continues to grow. Its facilities are spacious and aesthetic. Leadership abounds. Resources are rich and varied. Not even 4 million dollars of capital debt seems to daunt the enthusiasm of the people. Their energy level is high and contagious.

Who would have suspected trouble in River City's most aggressive and appealing church? Well, for one, I did not. Another consultant before me did not. We both missed what was happening the first time around. Luckily, I had a second chance. I learned from my experience with Transfiguration that even "healthy bodies" contract viruses. Second, the presence of the virus itself is not reason alone for it to be disruptive. It can either be enabled or contained. Finally, regardless of how healthy the exterior may look, the real health lies in "the body's" capacity to respond effectively.

The presenting problem at Transfiguration was tension among the nine-member staff. The consultant who preceded me addressed the tension through a plan of reorganization. After his exit, uneasiness persisted and became covert. Once the discomfort again rose to the surface, I responded to the staff's request to help enhance "communication" among the nine people. Within six months of my departure, the emotional edges that had been leveled reappeared. I received a second request to continue what I had started earlier. This time, however, I agreed to return only on the condition that we would focus on emotional processes.

At first, I was baffled. What was driving the emotionality? The most anxious people visibly were the program pastor and the minister of music. Their attention was riveted on the senior pastor. The "content" of their focus included his "Type A behavior," his unrelenting drive and "compulsivity," and his "power." More than the senior pastor knew, and therefore could acknowledge, he was anxious about their reactivity.

He hid it and somatized it (lower back pain, weight increase). To understand what was happening in the relationship system, we needed to make visible the emotional processes seeding the disease.

HISTORICAL CONDITIONS

For a decade Transfiguration had reflected its name—constantly changing its shape or form. "Success" was not without its stressors. (See table 6.1.)

Table 6.1

Timeline	Additions	Deletions	Stressors
2000	Major financial drive for a new sanctuary; addition of more than 100 members (600 total)		
2001	Addition of minister of education; addition of 80 new members		
2002	Addition of minister of youth		
2003	Continued membership growth (900 total)		
2004	Business manager added		
2005	Major financial drive for education center; addition of program pastor		
2006	Minister of music added; total membership at 1,400; contemporary worship introduced	Part-time organist/ choir director leaves	Several families leave, opposed to "all the change"
2007	Addition of minister of outreach; addition of preschool/ kindergarten director; membership at 1,800	Minister of youth leaves	Grief over minister of youth's departure
2008	Addition of executive pastor		
2009	Major financial drive to acquire additional land; membership exceeds 2,000		Division among church leaders concerning the many and rapid changes
2010	Five-year plan approved		Staff unrest

STRUCTURE AND FUNCTION

Diagram 6.1 below outlines the staff's shape with names, ages, and gender of each person.

The executive pastor (responsible for property and finances) and the program pastor (responsible for parish activities) were supervised by the senior pastor. The senior pastor's role had become designer of the future, primary preacher for worship services, and general overseer of the staff. He ran on "high octane," challenged others to operate with the same energy, yet he did not run over people. Overall, the individuals who joined the staff found his energy and innovative spirit attractive and infectious. How, then, I thought, could the "content" of their complaints be the true friction point?

Structure and Function

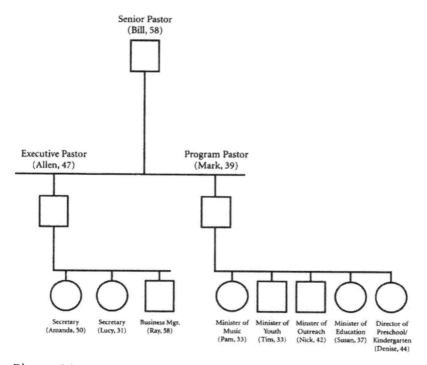

Diagram 6.1

THE VIRUS

I discovered the source of anxiety. What made its detection so difficult was that the virus came from outside the staff. The program pastor's wife felt threatened when the executive pastor joined the staff at a level equal to that of her husband. She hoped her husband would succeed as the senior pastor. She feared that the executive pastor would in time become entrenched and stand as a rival to her husband. The sooner the senior pastor left, the sooner her husband could replace him. She wanted the senior pastor ousted and fabricated "issues" to undermine him. She used her husband and her friend, the minister of music, as conduits for her anxiety. Infected, they carried her virus to other "cells," staff members and the personnel committee. Meanwhile the executive pastor and business manager overreacted to them and maintained the infection.

It would be simple to blame the program pastor's wife for all the pain. But that is cause-and-effect thinking, a non-systemic approach. People's actions are co-causal, subject to mutual forces; what other issues were contributing to staff unrest? For one thing, the staff members were already anxious about the senior pastor's high expectations of them. They also had anxiety about the constant change, and the new five-year plan indicated many shifts that lay ahead of them.

The senior pastor was engrossed with the new long-range plan. He thought he could just "weather the storm" and bolt ahead. But by absorbing their anxiety, he enabled it. How, we wonder, could this organizational "engine" lapse into being an emotional "sponge?" Being perceptive, he was quite aware of how the past changes and the future plans for change had been dazzling for some members but had a dizzying effect on others. He did not want to risk the momentum that had thrust the congregation forward. It is important to note, too, that he was the third of six children (all born within nine years, all but one male). He was making his mark in the world and receiving the recognition he always desired. He was not going to allow anything—particularly the foolishness of others—to endanger his position. More was happening, of course, than he knew. The program pastor's wife came from a very successful family. Her success was encased in her husband's. She needed him to shine, Thus two family systems and the drama of heroism collided.

The personnel committee—anxious about the staff's anxiety—also played a reinforcing role. The three of them loaded on the senior pastor to relieve their own anxiety. The executive pastor and business manager reacted to the programmatic staff members through distancing maneuvers.

ANXIETY'S FLOW

Notice the flow of anxiety among the staff members. (The presence of anxiety is noted by a jagged line, its flow by an arrow.) It begins with the program pastor and minister of music and is focused upon the senior pastor. The senior pastor ostensibly is calm, unnerved. But he internalizes his anxiety. (See Diagrams 6.2 and 6.3.)

The senior pastor listened and expressed his concern to the two unhappy souls but made no changes in his behavior, though there was a significant change in his body.

In Diagram 6.4, observe how anxiety keeps the relationship system "stuck together."

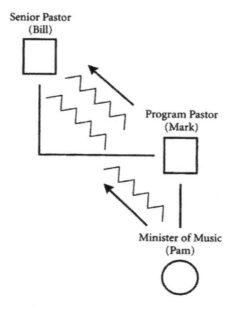

Diagram 6.2

Senior Pastor

Diagram 6.3

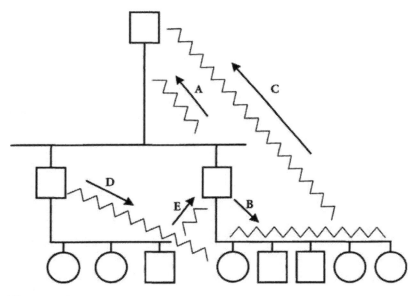

Diagram 6.4

Infected by his wife's anxiety, the program pastor (Mark) directs it toward the senior pastor (Bill)—Line A. Then, along with the minister of music (Pam), the program pastor generates anxiety among other staff members involved in programmatic activities. He questions the ability of the senior pastor to supervise. He impugns his motives, suggesting he is on an "ego trip." These staff members also turn their focus on the senior pastor (C). Meanwhile the executive pastor (Allen) turns reactive toward the minister of music (D) and the business manager

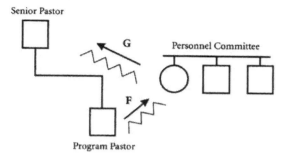

Diagram 6.5

focuses anxiously on the program pastor (B). Their reactivity takes the form of emotional cut-off (not talking, "the silent treatment").

To complicate matters, emotionality seeps into the personnel committee. The program pastor meets with them secretly to voice his displeasure with the senior pastor's "unilateral decisions" and "withdrawal from the staff" (F). Upset by his comments, the personnel committee transfers their anxiety to the senior pastor (G). (See Diagram 6.5.)

TRIANGLES REVISITED

The staff was tied up in its own emotionality. They were fastened together by a chain of triangles shown in Diagrams 6.6a–f.

As long as triangles exist, there is little chance for restoring balance. Triangles transmit anxiety; triangles relocate anxiety. Triangles are the globs of glue. They indicate that

people are not managing their anxiety;
people are stuck together in their anxiety;
change is inhibited.

People overlook the ways they maintain the problem that bedevils all of them. Unless they see how their own functioning binds them together, the system will not be free or unstuck. When one (or more) changes how they function, the glue loosens and the triangle cracks.

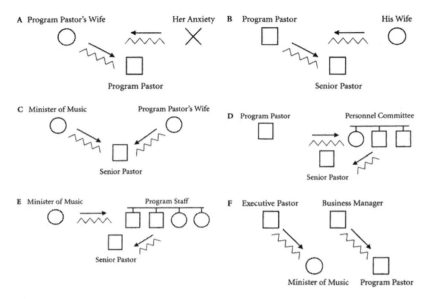

Diagram 6.6

BENIGN OR MALIGNANT

Friedman draws a parallel between disease processes and harmful emotional processes. He sees molecules and humans interacting in similar ways. The cells in our body specialize or differentiate. Mature cells limit their response to a special task, divide up labor among themselves, and take turns, thereby forming and sustaining the whole organism. Immature cells, however, live for themselves. A cancer cell, for example, has no capacity to regulate itself or to say "no" to itself. A cancer cell has no boundaries and respects no boundaries of other cells. Its most characteristic feature, Lewis Thomas states, is "that it lives only for itself." A cancer cell is "egocentric." Further, it is a parasite. It can't live except within the cell in which it starts its attack. It feeds on its host, drawing out the DNA of the living cell. A cancer cell replicates itself by depleting the cell from which it draws life. Ultimately it commits "biological suicide," destroying the living cell as well as itself because of its lack of differentiation.

Physician Paul Brand extends Friedman's notion to the Apostle Paul's analogy in 1 Corinthians 12, the comparison of the body of

Christ to the human body. Brand says that a cell can be either "egocentric" or "sociocentric," that is, it can either live only for itself or for the benefit of the whole. He "augments" Paul's analogy by substituting for the image of body parts the image of cells.

> The body is one unit, though it is made up of many cells, and though all its cells are many, they form one body. . . . If the white cell should say, because I am not a brain cell, I do not belong to the body, it would not for that reason cease to be part of the body. And if the muscle cell should say to the optic nerve cell, because I am not an optic nerve, I do not belong to the body, it would not for that reason cease to be a part of the body. If the whole body were an optic nerve cell, where would be the ability to walk? If the whole body were an auditory nerve, where would be the sense of sight? But in fact God has arranged the cells in the body, every one of them, just as He wanted them to be, If all cells were the same, where would the body be? As it is, there are many cells, but one body. (*Fearfully and Wonderfully Made*)

A cell may cling only to itself and live in the body, drawing benefits from it but contributing nothing to it, like a cancer cell. A cancer cell, Lewis points out, "de-differentiates"; it is "boundary-less." It invades and violates the integrity of other cells. When such cells replicate, there is malignancy—a deadly conflict and loss of integrity. If the growth of cancerous cells can be localized, it is benign. The anxious staff members and the personnel committee at Transfiguration de-differentiate. They react against each other rather than define themselves to one another. They enable the disease process through their own emotionality. Unable to manage their anxiety, they tighten the circle, lose a sense of perspective, and shift their anxious burden, all of which is malignant.

DETECTION AND TREATMENT

How can the disease process be recognized in relationship systems? First, look for where the virus of anxiety begins and how it is reinforced. People lacking differentiation will spread the disease. They will focus on others, not themselves. They will diagnose others. They will invade others, making unfounded or reckless charges against them. Further, they will not move toward peaceful agreement or balance. It is the nature of viruses to replicate themselves. In practical terms, they want to prevail. They want to gain votes or support for their position.

How can we treat the disease process? Like cancer, there can be surgery. Extract the cancerous growth—"Kick the bums out!" There can be chemotherapy. Hold the infection in check—"Let's make rules!" Or there can be a strengthening of the host cells so that the virus cannot gain a foothold, that is, increase people's immune capacities. The immune capacity in relationship systems is the capacity to define the self. To paraphrase Martin Luther, "Here I stand. I can do no other. It is neither good nor right to go against reason and conscience, or one's own integrity."

Friedman warns against two typical treatments: blood transfusion and changing the chairs on the Titanic. Both are often used as "cures" in anxious relationship systems. Viruses are impervious to "new blood." Viruses are not contained by "shuffling the deck"—or the deck chairs, since there is a leak in the hull or cell membrane. I would add a third typical treatment that is ineffective: "benign neglect." It is treating a virus by hoping that it'll go away by itself or by sweeping its presence under the rug and out of awareness. Benign neglect only gives opportunity to malignant processes. It is an escape from taking responsibility. People have to change how they *function* when the hull is leaking.

The keys to treatment, Friedman suggests, are the leaders. They are *positioned* to be the church family's "differentiation," the immune cells of the whole. They are the body's mature cells. They function as the anti-globules or the de-gluers. Leaders are responsible for defining themselves and ensuring the group's definition of who they are.

Chapter 7

Being a Prophet Is Nice Work—
If You Can Find a Job

Without difference, there is no relation, just mixture, and without distance, nothing to which we can raise our eyes.

—D. M. Dooling

The lover must lose himself in order to find himself—not to lose himself.

—Kurt Wolff

The main problem is not differences in points of view; it is the emotional reaction to the differences.

—Michael Nichols

A MATTER OF SPACE

Indeed, as it is said, a prophet is without honor in his own country. In fixed surroundings you eat the same food, play the same games, talk about the same weather, pay the same piper. A prophet, though, stands out from the sameness, dreaming new dreams or speaking strange words. "You have heard it said of old, but I say unto you . . ." The prophet gets strong direction for living from his own beliefs and goals. The prophet challenges the country's foundation. "That is a dead idea; and this is a disguise." Truly, the messenger runs the risk of losing more than honor. The "stuck together" forces of sameness cannot tolerate anyone who sticks their neck out too far: "He's a loose cannon: he's stretched the limit."

It almost sounds too dramatic, yet there is accuracy in claiming that anytime we self-differentiate from the group's intactness, we are in the prophet's *functioning* position. We stand out, not contemptuously (cutoff), but at a distance sufficient to shed new light. An anxious group might react to our separateness as too much distancing or as a move *against* or *outside* of them:

> "How could you do that to us? We wouldn't do that to you."
> "Are you crazy? No one in their right mind would do that."
> "We are a happy group; we'll have none of that behavior."

These voices will try to pull us back to the old arrangement and familiar ways of functioning. Some might punish our self-differentiation by a distancing of their own. When we self-differentiate, the more mature people will have their own differentiating capacities tapped and elevated. The less mature will cut off or squeeze tighter.

JERUSALEM AND CANA

We can self-differentiate, but we can't prevent people from distancing or fusing with us. For instance, the Gospel writer describes Jesus as knowing from whom he had come and to where he was going, and then taking a towel to wash the disciples' feet. Well-defined and well-directed, Jesus enacts a parable of the self-giving that is to come. Later, though, he sets his face toward Jerusalem for his ultimate self-giving, and the crowds start to dwindle. At the site of the crucifixion, only one of the disciples is reported to be present. In the aftermath all but one of the disciples are huddled together in a locked room like frightened children. Anxious people always make adjustments in "space." The individuals above "vote with their feet," withdrawing and disengaging. They have widened the space. But narrowing the space is also a maneuver of anxious people. Early in the ministry of Jesus, when the guests at the Cana wedding feast drain the wineskins, Mary, in a whirl of worry, tells her son that there is no wine. Not entrapped by her anxiety, Jesus says his hour has not yet come. A bit later, an excited crowd rushes forward to make Jesus a king, but he retreats from their emotional intensity. His kingdom, he says, is not of this world. Fusing or closing the space between people is another behavior of people who do not manage their anxiety well.

AND ROME AND SALEM

The astronomer Galileo Galilei (1564–1642) constructed the first complete telescope. He used it to collect data in support of Copernicus's theory that the earth revolved around the sun, not vice-versa. But the theologians of the day insisted on the centrality of the earth. They had previously condemned the theory as inimical to the teaching of the Roman Catholic Church. Warned not to advance the theory, Galileo defied the admonition with the 1632 publication of his treatise on the two great world systems. He was tried as a heretic and forced to denounce his belief. He spent his last eight years blind and under house arrest.

A half-century later on another continent, the same anxious forces were at work in the witch trials of Salem, Massachusetts. While the origins of the panic are contested, scholars have discussed how occult practices and fears of demons had a profound effect on this highly superstitious culture. As one story goes, the daughter of a minister and her cousin were so physically overcome by tales of the supernatural that a physician diagnosed them as "bewitched." Many of the accused "witches" were brought to trial. Those who admitted to witchcraft were spared; those who adhered to their innocence were hanged. Anxiety had spawned and filled the town with potential witches. As the craze finally came to an end, several young girls who claimed to have had seizures came upon a lady in nearby Ipswich. Believing the elderly woman was a witch, the girls went into convulsions. In Ipswich, however, there was little interest in witches. The girls were not asked for names or details, lost their frenzy, and went on their way. The witch hunt ended, but not before many people had lost their lives and countless others who had been accused had been jailed, or lost their land, and livelihoods.

Retrospectively, we wonder how such immature and cruel behaviors could have happened, much less have been tolerated. But identical processes take place in families, neighborhoods, schools, workplaces, and churches. We find it difficult to face difference, distance, and hard choice. When our relationships are based on a cozy closeness or a "pudding of sameness," we encounter even greater difficulty. Threatened, we make adjustments in "space." We push the panic buttons, close the hatches, censor the books, pass regulatory measures, hold rallies to wave flags, throw verbal bricks, and abandon sinking ships. We can be immature. The stories cited above are mirrors for us to look at—and ponder.

CHANGE THROUGH DEFINITION

Let us look at a church family that moved from reactivity to response. We will learn how some anxious people made adjustments in their "space," resorting to secrecy and pursuit behavior. We will also recognize how some people differentiated themselves and restored calm. Trinity Church is a 1500-member congregation. In the last decade it has increased its numbers 20 percent. It is located in an area of older homes inhabited by many old-timers and many new professional families. Five years ago it embarked on a building program, erecting a family life center to accommodate its fresh growth. This was the first major capital expense for the congregation in twenty years. While the center was being built, the congregation was jolted by the resignation of a popular staff member who was suspected of sexual misconduct. Within several weeks the congregation suffered a second significant blow. The chairperson of the building committee disappeared when it became known that the contractor for the center had other business interests with the chairperson. Rumors persisted that the chairperson received a "payoff" from the contractual arrangement. Some of the old-timers who had opposed the new addition grumbled even more.

Seventeen months after these events and twelve months after the completion of the facility, Pastor Shaw came to see me. A few days before his visit with me, he learned that a petition had been circulated requesting that he step down as the head pastor. He had been a member of the clergy for almost twenty-five years, fourteen of which he had served at Trinity. Part of our initial conversation follows.

Shaw: I don't understand it. Things have been tough with all of the shocks we have had. But no one blamed me. No one was after my neck.
Steinke: Who is passing the petition around for signatures?
Shaw: That's the real perplexing thing . . . shocking, unexpected. From what I've been told, it's Anna Parker. We've been friends for

years . . . had Thanksgiving dinner with her family . . . always supportive of me, always dependable. My wife and I are really hurt and feel betrayed.

Steinke: What's happening in her life? Do you know?

Shaw: Nothing . . . but what difference does that make?

Steinke: A lot. What's happening?

Shaw: You see this is what is so disturbing. About eight months ago she lost her job. Fired. Had been an executive secretary for a company, well-paid. She's sixty-one; she'll never get a job like that again. I consoled her, supported her, stood beside her . . . now this dagger in the back.

Steinke: Not too surprising, is it?

Shaw: What do you mean?

Steinke: What I mean is that there is no difference between deifying you or crucifying you.

Shaw: There is to me.

Steinke: But not for Anna. Either way she's been overfocused on you. Now she's exchanged honeymoon tactics for blackmail tactics.

Shaw: Obviously. But it affects me . . . truthfully, scares me.

Steinke: Sounds like a golden opportunity for growth.

Shaw: Come on. I came here to feel better, to get out of this mess.

Steinke: I'm not Dr. Feelgood.

Shaw: Great! I came here for help. I've got a mortgage, a son in college, a reputation at stake.

Steinke: I'll be your coach. There's an old saying that there are no great therapists, only great patients.

Shaw: You're saying it's up to me.

Steinke: You learn quickly.

Shaw: Yeah. But I don't like confrontation.

Steinke: Do you like being stepped on?

Shaw: I'm one of those passive-aggressive clergy. I swallow my anger.

Steinke: Do you like being stepped on?

Shaw: I don't want to hassle. Why me? This isn't going to be painless.

Steinke: Why not you? You're a perfect foil for Anna.

Shaw: She wouldn't be doing this, you mean, to someone who'd stand up to her. Oh, boy. Her husband knuckles under to her. Her daughter dances to her tune. Some people at church cater to her.

Steinke: So her boss "one ups" her. Do you want her to pin her pain on you when it belongs somewhere else?

Shaw: I don't get it. Of all the people in the world . . . me. I'm mixed up, too. You know, being all things to all people, that stuff.

Steinke: Does that mean you must be a sitting duck for hunters? A Goliath
   for any sling shot?
Shaw: I don't know what anything means anymore. Well, I've got to be fair
   and understanding.
Steinke: If you're playing with a full deck. . . . Sounds to me like someone
   shuffled the deck when you weren't looking.
Shaw: She's had a tough go of it. She's out of line; she's stretched it.
Steinke: And you say you're passive-aggressive. Who's got the problem?

I like Shaw. I believed he had energy, though at this time it was governing him negatively. He had the capacity to let his pain motivate him.
What he lacked in order to take risks was self-definition.

OVERFOCUS

Shaw is no different from most of us when we are confused and hurt—
and passive. He's just as overfocused on Anna as she is on him. When
we are overfocused, we close the space between ourselves and others.
We're connected too tightly. Inevitably, overfocus is a clear sign that
anxiety—converted into reactive grumbling—is related to other relationships in the life of the complainer. Both Anna's and Shaw's overfocus are signs of the same phenomenon.

Anna's conversion from deifying to crucifying is the same process—
overfocusing. People can put us on a pedestal or in a dumpster. Either
way, there's insufficient emotional distance. I'm sure that Rev. Shaw
had contributed to his place on Mt. Olympus just as he was about to
reinforce his position in Anna's nether world. Symptom and response
are connected. Though her criticism is a symptom stemming from
another condition in her life, it alone could not create conflict. Anxious
reactivity requires feedback. Anxiety is bipolar.

Pursuit behavior is any behavior that overfocuses on another person.
The most obvious form of such behavior is rescue. If we are intent on
saving or fixing someone, we take too much responsibility for their
lives. Rescuers can't tolerate healthy distance between themselves and
others. Rev. Shaw verges on it when he makes excuses for Anna's
behavior. Unable to bear her pain, he becomes anxious in its presence.
It's hardly genuine care for Anna. It is actually his own anxiety active
in reduction of itself.

By far the most difficult form of pursuit behavior to recognize is criticism. How can those who act adversarially be said to be in pursuit? We feel alienated, not close. But criticism is characterized by overfocus. The "stinger" and the "stung" are *emotionally* connected. Whenever a gnawing critic gets inside our brain cells and we can't expunge him, we are connected, even if negatively. Whenever someone gets under our skin, we are infected with anxiety. If we are reactive to a pursuer, the pursuit behavior achieves its goal: connection. Strange as it sounds, the critic wants to be close. After all, if we can't be close through play, ecstasy, touch, and nurture, our only option to accomplish closeness is through angry outbursts, specious charges, or harsh accusations. People feel close to us when they know we are thinking about them. *What* we think is not as important as *that* we are thinking about them. We play into the hands of criticizers when we react to their invasion rather than define ourselves to it.

UNDERGROUND MURMURING

A number of times in the New Testament, we find the Greek word *goggizo*. One of its meanings is to speak secretly or in a whisper. We find it happening in the church family when people talk about, not to others. Secrecy is an inevitable part of anxious blaming. Anna Parker's petition was a behind-the-back operation. Pastor Shaw discovered later that she and seven or eight others had conducted a series of secret meetings. Interestingly, he told me that two of the individuals were greatly distressed when the staff member resigned for sexual misconduct. They were enthusiastic supporters of him. Two other members of the secret meetings were both outspoken critics of the new center and the sources of many rumors concerning the building chairperson's questionable financial dealings.

Secrecy is anxious reactivity. It only produces more anxiety. Secrets, therefore, are generators of triangles. A tells B about C. A and B know. C does not know; C is placed in the *outside* position. And if A and B are secretly anxious and anxiously secret who knows what reactivity will follow and who else will be targeted for the C position? Generally, someone who is secretive about a third person is secretive about himself. Further, secret gatherings seldom seek the welfare of the whole community. Obviously they are not dialogical.

It is secrecy itself, not the content of the secrets, that is harmful. Secret meetings neglect the evangelical counsel "to speak the truth in love." In the New Testament, three situations address disturbed relationships in the Christian community: the Matthean sayings (Matthew 5:21–24, 7:3, 18:15–22), the Council of Jerusalem (Acts 15), and the chaos at Corinth (1 Corinthians 1:12, 3:4). In Matthew 18 the counsel is to "go and tell" an offending brother his fault "between you and him alone." Acts 15 contains the account of the leaders of the early church who meet to settle the conflicting opinions regarding the Gentiles and circumcision. The Council decides to send two representatives to convey to the Gentile Christians that circumcision will not be expected of them. At the church in Corinth, people had divided into clashing subgroups, some claiming to belong to Paul, some to Apollo, some to Cephas. The apostle Paul urges them not to be "puffed up in favor of one against another."

Although we know today that secrets are a telltale characteristic of dysfunctional families, we often protect and refuse to expose irresponsible whisperers. Thus many responsible people, by not facing up to the secrecy, participate in another kind of secrecy: secrecy about the secrecy. It's all very anxious behavior.

FROM CONVICTION TO DEFINITION

Consider these statements:

> "Here I stand!"
> "Give me liberty or give me death."
> "The buck stops here."
> "I have a dream."

All these statements are thought-out expressions of personal boundaries and convictions. The individuals who uttered the statements were defining themselves in their relationships with others. They were acting on the courage of their own conviction instead of on the basis of emotional reactivity. They differentiated themselves from the reactive pressures of the emotional system. Their convictions did not set them above or against others. They defined themselves *to* others. Through convictions and belief, the self-defined know who they are and where they are going. They develop specific goals. They are not easily rattled by the reactivity of others. Beliefs are binders of anxiety.

Pastor Shaw worked with me for about a year, and diligently. He turned his focus to his own functioning. The brouhaha simmered after five or six months. Anna Parker's secret society went out of business for lack of reinforcement. Furthermore, the leaders of the congregation established and communicated a new policy on criticism; they reworked the standards of evaluation for the pastor with clear, objective goals; they reaffirmed their commitment to the goal of mission and ministry to the realities of their neighborhood. Shaw's self-differentiation activated or raised that of others.

I had given Shaw a formula, $b=f$ (p.e.), devised by field theorist Kurt Lewin. Translated, it means "Behavior is a function of the transaction of personality and environment." We can change the person, and the environment changes, and we can change the environment and the person changes. Person and context are mutual influences. They form a system. Initially Pastor Shaw expressed skepticism and instead was bent on changing the environment or the attackers. But he began to change how he functioned and the environment changed. He recognized that the dislocations of the last several years had changed the church's environment, which in turn had changed the people's mood and outlook. Life is all of a piece.

Pastor Shaw's effectiveness in differentiating self from others helped me to envision the continuum that exists between undifferentiation and differentiation. In table 7.1, I note the continuum that characterizes low to high functioning. It is significant to note that the only way to increase our functioning in a differentiated manner is in the midst of forces that fight against it—anxiety, hostility, immaturity, and dependency. We sharpen our objectivity with those who criticize us, our imagination with those who challenge us, and our definition with those who would define us.

Undifferentiation is promoted by the emotional system that encourages people to give up themselves on behalf of the group. In such a system, much thinking and decision making are emotionally based and designed to allay anxiety of the moment. Such an adaptation gives power to those who take the least responsibility for their lives. Lewis Thomas has noted that social animals become qualitatively different creatures when assembled in groups than when alone or in pairs. Simple locusts, for example, are meditative, quiet things, yet when

Table 7.1

Undifferentiated	*Differentiated*
1. Quickly offended, easily provoked, too sensitive, slow to recover	1. Self-managing, shapes environment, resourceful
2. Reactive, instinctive, automatic	2. Responsive, intentional, thoughtful
3. Underhanded, covert, flourishes in the dark	3. Open, light-shedding, aware
4. Demanding, willful, stubborn, resistant (especially to reason and love), unbending	4. Resilient, has sense of proportion
5. Think in black/white or yes/no, intolerant of ambiguity, seek final solution, want all or nothing	5. Have breadth of understanding, allow time for things to process
6. Blame, criticize, displace, fault-finding, have poor discrimination	6. Take responsibility for self, learn when challenged, define self from within self
7. Uptight, serious, defensive	7. Relaxed, at ease, sensible
8. Competitive, either with or against, see life as a contest, contemptuous	8. Take turns, collaborate, stay in touch even when tension grows
9. Vague, non-specific, cloaked	9. Clear, objective, purposeful
10. Create too much or too little space and one-sided solutions	10. Create space, options, and common goals

locusts gather together, they "become excited, change colors, undergo endocrine revisions, and intensify their activity," according to Thomas. When a sufficient number of them are packed tightly in a group, they vibrate, hum, and take off like a jet airliner. Many church families, caught in anxiety, are not much different from the locusts. In contrast, more differentiated persons can participate freely in the emotional field without the fear of becoming too fused with others. Less automatic, they use their awareness and hold their ground when things fly apart.

Chapter 8

What Shall It Profit a Parish If It Gets over the Hump but Falls into the Abyss?

You cannot solder an Abyss with Air.

—Emily Dickinson

Distress and pain are friends to growth.

—Augustus Napier

Unless a grain of wheat falls into the earth and dies, it remains alone; but if it dies, it bears much fruit.

—John 12:24

MATURITY

Automatic processes are designed for survival. They serve us best in the short run or for emergencies. If a person or group relies solely or consistently on these processes, the very survival that is sought is undermined. Automatic behavior is the hallmark of immature people. Bent on survival, they accept few challenges and experience little growth. Immature people react with a small part of themselves to a small part of their world. They limit themselves by paying attention only to what is close up, by focusing on the moment, and by posturing in defense. Essentially, they let the things around them inform and shape their lives.

Maturity increases survival. For the long haul, reflection and resilience are needed. Mature people respond with a large part of themselves to a large part of their world. They move beyond limiting conditions by seeing what might yet be, by allowing time for things to process, and by responding with self-control and poise. They have a greater capacity to modify and shape their environment.

The immaturity-maturity continuum plays a prominent role in how we interpret stressors and what responses we make to them. Church families have their own maturity levels. And I have not yet worked with a church family, pressured by its own anxiety, that has been able to rise above its maturity level. Before we examine two congregations representing the low and the high ends of the continuum, let me illustrate the intersecting of the continuum with various levels of stress. (See Diagram 8.1.)

The space between the two lines indicates that as the degree of maturity increases there is a wider range of responses, a larger view of things, and a longer span of time allowed for processing what is happening. (See Diagram 8.2.)

By adding a vertical line to depict the strength of a stressor, we can visualize its impact along the continuum. (See Diagram 8.3.)

A stressor of B strength (low severity) affects someone at level 1; a stressor of F strength (high severity) affects someone at level 4.

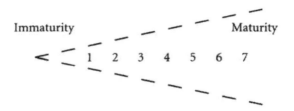

Diagram 8.1

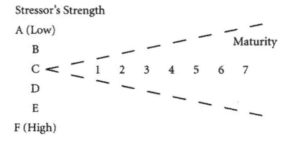

Diagram 8.2

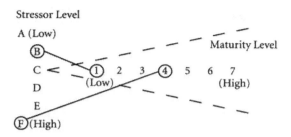

Diagram 8.3

What generally happens is that level 1 people inflate the B stressor. Its "critical mass" is enlarged beyond its reality. A house is on fire and they shout, "The town is burning down." Immature people are more reactive. Being reactive, they also take longer to recover from stress and suffer from it more frequently. In the situation above, chances are that the B stressor on level 1 will appear to be more severe than the F stressor on the more mature (level 4). The more mature have ample resources, take time to address the stressor, and use imagination to handle their stress. They have greater balancing capacities. Another aspect to consider is where people focus their attention. Level 1 people attend to the stressor, the vertical line, the *conditions* out there. Level 4 people direct more attention to their own choices, strengths, and options.

SIMILAR YET DIFFERENT

Why do church families with similar conditions produce different outcomes? Why do some suffer, others adapt? What determines whether a relationship system works through its emotional processes for the better or for the worse? Many variables are involved, but none more than the system's general level of maturity. Table 8.1 lists contrasting characteristics of the immature and mature.

Immature church families want to get over the hump. They are blind to the abyss. Fiercely intent on fixing or removing the condition or stressor, they mistake the disappearance of the *symptom* for the cure. And each time another symptom appears, they see only the hump. They remove it again, oblivious to the deeper chasm and the strength of emotional processes. They try to solder the Abyss with air. But there is no

Table 8.1

Immature	*Mature*
1. Believe in a final solution	1. Accept proximate solutions to insolvable problems
2. Impatient, quick on the trigger, rash, demand "Now!"	2. Deliberate, reflective, able to wait, hold "now-not yet" in tension
3. Want to settle scores, receive restitution	3. Seek support from others
4. Rely on cause-and-effect thinking and either/or approach	4. Use systematic thinking and codetermined interaction, recognize mutual forces at play
5. Deny problem, deny outside help is needed	5. Acknowledge impasse, open to objective appraisal
6. Look for a lightning rod (someone to blame, manipulate)	6. Look for due process
7. Hyper-vigilant, secretive	7. Rethink the future, set clear goals
8. Too serious, adopt "Worry wart" role	8. Loosen grip, relax, find some "breathing holes"
9. Cry "Dumb luck" and "Nobody cares," see themselves as victims	9. Ask "What can I do?"
10. Have as a theme "More smoke"	10. Have as a theme "More light"
11. Vague, indefinite about choices	11. Make clear decisions, take specific actions

profit, no gain, or no change—only new symptoms, another hump, or a revived condition of stress.

THE DIFFERENCE THAT MAKES A DIFFERENCE

Let's look at two congregations experiencing the same conditions but producing different outcomes. One gets over the hump but falls into its own Abyss. The other sees its own Abyss but avoids a fall into it. (See table 8.2.)

Both congregations shared common characteristics and were involved in situations that were alike. Their pastoral staff of four had been reduced to one associate minister. At Unity the associate was a thirty-four-year-old male, married with two children, who had been there for

Table 8.2

	Common Conditions	
	Unity Church	*Community Church*
Membership	1,301	1,290
Annual Budget	$681,000	$652,000
Church Staff (full-time)	4	4
Losses	Founding pastor retires after 27 years. Retired missionary and wife killed in auto accident (very active and respected members for seven years). Associate pastor resigns after sexual affair with minor. Chairperson of congregation suffers the loss of his 17-year-old son by suicide.	Founding pastor retires after 22 years. Three current leaders and three former leaders die in 19-month period. Associate pastor resigns (was to be heir to founding pastor).
Lawsuits	Parents of minor sue church	Associate pastor sues church
Average Age of Membership	34.2	32.1
Percent of Budget for Benevolence	17%	19%

three years. He was an easy-going, good-natured individual and eager to be considered for the head pastor's role. Community Church's associate was a thirty-seven-year-old single female, divorced for twelve years with one child. She excelled in people skills and provided a caring ministry. In both cases, the associates were named to the lists of potential candidates to succeed the retired pastors. The ways in which the congregations handled their circumstances diverged in several significant ways. (See table 8.3.)

Everyone can imagine that there were indeed other nuances and forces at work in these church families. From these preliminary facts, though, we can already see that Unity is headed for a showdown. While not everything "came up roses" at Community, they were still managing things with clarity and direction.

What happened next? The associate at Unity received the position as senior pastor. A dozen members left in protest. A settlement was

Table 8.3

Unity	*Community*
1. The retired pastor remained a member of Unity and was vague about his future relationship with the church. He kept his fingers in the pot, especially by serving as a behind-the-scenes lobbyist for the associate to become his successor.	1. The retired pastor left with several clearly defined boundaries: joining another congregation for a period of three years, attending only special festival services and annual events at Community. A year before he left, he guided the congregation in a self-study and prepared it for the transition. A five-year plan was developed.
2. The "Old Guard" supported the associate's candidacy; however, a mixture of old and new members ("New Guard") wanted the church to seek an "experienced" pastor.	2. The Transition Team developed guidelines for the selection of the new pastor in view of the five-year plan. The associate was not among the finalists. Many felt her skills were best suited for her current responsibilities.
3. Factions emerged. Several strategy meetings were held by each side.	3. Disappointed that the associate did not make the list of final candidates, some members requested the Transition Team to consider women for the post as all the finalists were men. The Transition Team accepted their counsel and extended for another 60 days the search for at least two female candidates.
4. The Old Guard held most of the elected positions and wanted the role of pastor filled as soon as possible, at least before the annual election. The New Guard, sensing their tactics, formed a protest bloc. Each side became increasingly adamant in its positions.	4. The associate agreed to offer her resignation contingent upon the wishes of the new pastor.

reached out of court with the parents of the minor sexually involved with a former associate. The retired pastor offered his services as a part-time assistant to his successor, who accepted the offer. Another group of thirty to forty people left, complaining of the retired pastor's meddle-some behavior. A group of equal size opposed the pretrial arrangement and withheld their offerings. Within fifteen months the new senior pastor was under fire from a "remnant" of the New Guard. At this point I was asked to intervene.

Meanwhile, Community narrowed its candidate list to two finalists, both males. The one who openly expressed that he wanted the female associate to remain was chosen to be the new pastor. Prior to his arrival, the new pastor received approval to hire a consultant to help the pastors and leaders in the first year of transition and in the light of recent losses. I worked with the pastors and leaders for a year. They were well on their way toward implementing their plans.

The individuals who invited me to come to Unity consisted mostly of the Old Guard. Not enamored with outside help, they had little choice, as losses of members and financial support were mounting. But they were prepared to sabotage the process. They thought that they could blame their troubles on the "others," or "sore losers" as they referred to the New Guard (what was left of it). When I introduced systems concepts and started talking about focusing on self and not others, on process and not content, they informed me that I wasn't helping them and they needed another kind of resource person. They wanted to get over the hump, not get well. Sadly, in two and a half years their ranks shrank from 1,301 to 780.

There are no shortcuts in managing emotional processes, particularly painful ones. Preoccupied with "getting beyond it all" or "getting out of the mess," the church family operates for the short run. Automatic and reactive behaviors prevail. I have learned from my experience that by speeding up the recovery process, I maintain people's anxiety. To help anxious systems I need to be a "nonanxious presence," willing to be patient, as the process is worked out and completed.

THE SHARKS OR WHAT

Friedman tells the story of a man who had a rare form of cancer and needed surgery. The survival rate for the surgery was 20 percent. The feisty patient said that he wanted to be part of the 20 percent. He proceeded with the surgery without prior consultation with family or friends. He was back at work in a month. Friedman asked the man if he had ever heard about the USS Cruiser *Indianapolis*. He hadn't, and Friedman told him the story. After delivering the atom bomb, the cruiser sank in the Pacific. Struck suddenly by enemy fire, the ship went under and released 800 soldiers into the ocean. Before long, sharks encircled them. Every so often a soldier would swim toward the sharks and give himself up. How, Friedman asked, could the man explain why some survived. "Those guys who swam away," the man replied, "they didn't have no future."

I thought of this story when one of my clients came to see me for psychotherapy. Both her physicians and psychiatrist had told her that there was nothing more they could do for her. In search of relief for her chronic pain, they had exhausted numerous tests and medication. She had to talk to someone. For almost two years, Sheila had suffered physically and mentally, at times sleeping or lying down for long periods. During the early therapy sessions, she talked in generalities, exhibited minimal affect, and showed disinterest. Gradually she made progress. Her pain became more intermittent.

Sheila had been over-functioning for years, blindly and automatically taking care of her children's, her husband's, and the congregation's needs. She had so denied her own needs; she could hardly identify one. Her body, through the signal of pain, was sending a message. Her exaggerated caretaking blanketed awareness of her own needs, until the psyche in concert with the body delivered symptoms. In one session I told her Friedman's story of the cruiser and the sharks. A portion of our conversation follows.

Sheila: You mean to tell me I've been swimming to the sharks?
Pete: Big ones.
Sheila: That's terrible. Wait 'til I tell Michael. [Her husband] No, I won't tell Michael [laughter]. He'll think you're crazy and I'm crazy.
Pete: Are you going to keep taking care of Michael? He loves it.
Sheila: Why do I do that?
Pete: Is that important? I'm wondering if you can live without sharks. Don't you need to feed them?
Sheila: No, not anymore. I'm going to have a future.

Incidentally, as Sheila started to conclude her therapy, she mentioned: "I only hurt now on Sundays." She was learning to focus on Sheila's response instead of automatically attending to everyone's needs.

RESTORING BALANCE

Under threat we act automatically. Survival is everything. We slide toward the immature side of the continuum. We are impatient. We blame, relieving our own pain by focusing it on others. We use either/or thinking. "Stuck" in our anxiety, we err on the side of shortsightedness. The goal is to get over the hump.

How can we shift to the other side of the continuum? What is most helpful in achieving management of our stressful situation? How can we restore balance? I have noted below a list of ten actions that keep a group on the side of growth.

1. Having a plan
2. Expressing problems in terms of relationships
3. Knowing what triggers anxiety
4. Handling anxiety on the level of consciousness
5. Being willing to invest in what is going to be
6. Identifying strengths and resources
7. Creating options
8. Remaining on the side of challenge (toleration of pain, threat, sabotage)
9. Following the plan
10. Asking questions.

Chapter 9

Remembering the Future

No wind serves him who addresses his voyage to no certain point.
—Seneca

If the blind lead the blind, both shall fall into the ditch.
—Matthew 15

Time is nature's way of keeping everything from happening at once.
—Graffiti

DIRECTION AND DEFINITION

"Not much happens without a dream," Robert Greenleaf says, "and for something great to happen there must be a great dream." He believes the leader of a group must design a picture of the future. By articulating a sense of where a group is going, the leader gives it a direction and a destiny. Peter Senge of MIT's Sloan School of Management has also identified the leader as the "steward of the vision." The leader advances the vision through steady oversight. What matters most, Senge adds, is not so much what the vision is as what the vision does. The vision is the group's way of defining itself and chartering its purpose. Friedman would not argue with either one, as he envisions the leader to be the one who can most fire the group's imaginative capacities. But he would carefully note that the vision that defines the group must be forged and

103

safeguarded by leaders who are themselves well differentiated. The vision, in other words, cannot be severed from the visionaries. Before anyone can be a "steward of the vision," one must be a "steward of the self." Being a dreamer and overseer are effective roles to the degree that the leader functions with integrity and promotes responsibility in others. The leader achieves this by defining self, regulating one's own anxiety, staying connected to others, stimulating their resources, and staying the course.

All biological organisms need a *direction* to function effectively. They need a "head" to ensure that the organism is "headed" somewhere. Using a chinchilla and an elephant as examples, Friedman notes that the head of each has the same effect on the rest of the body, though the heads are connected to immensely different bodies. The head directs. In social organisms the same arrangement is needed for effective functioning. The leader functions as the director of the group. This does not mean that the leader dominates, that is, forces the many parts to dance to the leader's directives. Rather, it is the leader's function to *affect* the group so that their resources are energized and their functions are promoted. In effect, this is how the organ of the brain interacts with the other organs of the body. Because of the leader's *position* in the system, it is the leader who can most affect calm, focus, and change in the group.

COMMUNITY NEEDS IMMUNITY

Friedman offers a novel way of understanding leadership. He draws a parallel between our physical bodies and our relationship systems. Cellular processes, he states, are the same at all levels of life. He believes that human beings relate to one another in the same way that biological cells respond to one another. Specifically, he sees a likeness between the immune processes at work in our bodies and the self-differentiation processes at work in our relationships. Further, he believes the immune response of the community lies with its leaders. By examining his ideas more closely, we can learn much about both handling anxious reactivity and promoting health in the church family.

Lewis Thomas has explained the importance of the immune system. On the one hand there is no such thing as an isolated being. Life is a web of connectedness. On the other hand he recognizes that "given the chance under the right condition," any cell (insect, animal, or human) making contact with any other cell, even if foreign, will fuse with it. *Cell fusion* disclaims the significance of "specificity, integrity, and separateness in living things." But immunity affirms it. The purpose of the immune system is to separate self from non-self. The white cells or lymphocytes in our bodies are designed to protect us from irritating or toxic agents. They serve as the "palace guard" or the "armed forces" of the body. They turn away or kill foreign invaders that are hostile to our well-being. They protect us from viruses and other harmful microorganisms. With keen discriminatory powers, the white cells distinguish between genetically identical tissue and genetically alien material. They possess an incredible sense of belonging. To have a successful skin graft or a life-saving organ transplant, surgeons must suppress the immune processes that would otherwise spurn the foreign tissue. Even then, the donor's organ must have a high degree of genetic match to that of the recipient.

THE FAILURE OF RESPONSE

The immune system is our biological salvation. Nonetheless, it can also be our ruin. If the immune system is immature, weak, and undeveloped, it cannot provide the needed sensitization against toxins. If, for example, a three-year-old imbibes ten ounces of Jack Daniels whiskey, the youngster is not immunologically ready to fight the virulence of alcohol. The hard liquor is an invader, a deadly one at that. If a thirty-year-old drinks ten ounces, it might feel like death, but it does not induce it.

It is reported that Europeans killed more Native Americans through disease than bloodshed. Native Americans lacked the immune response necessary to resist the new microbes introduced by the invading Europeans. But few diseases spread from the Native Americans to the Europeans. Why? The answer is related to the fact that animals breed viruses. For centuries, Europeans had domesticated and lived with animals in thickly populated pockets, whereas Native Americans domesticated few animals and lived in thinner density. Their situation did not require the mobilization of immunity against certain animal-bred viruses.

Our immune cells may fail us if they lack the power of discrimination. Lymphocytes can show up with no ability to distinguish between self and non-self. Therefore viruses defy inhibition, and they multiply.

There is also evidence that social conditions reduce immune function. States of grief, loneliness, and stress impair the activity of the immune cells. One researcher, who studied men's immune response following the death of their wives, found that the white cells did not change during bereavement but behaved differently. The cells did not perform their regular function, acting as if they themselves were mourning. Other studies have discovered a similar relationship between lower immunity and victim thinking, self-loathing, and emotional strain.

UNRESPONSIVENESS

If leaders are to function in the same fashion as the immune system, we need to reflect on the implications. Immature (hesitant and undifferentiated) leaders exhibit weak powers of discrimination. They make no response when a response is needed (similar to the position of emotional cutoff). The "Jack Daniels" of the congregation simply overpowers them, nullifying their function and impact. With no one determining and monitoring what is and what is not acceptable or who is or who is not responsible, noxious agents spread their poison of unfounded charges, self-centered demands, or aggressive threats. The symptoms that develop in the church family (heated argument, antagonistic behavior, cutting remarks, and exiting maneuvers) are not unlike those displayed by our diseased bodies (fever, coughing, bleeding, and diarrhea). But the anxiously reactive are always *encouraged* by passive leaders, or, in Winston Churchill's observation, "The malice of the wicked is equal to the weakness of the virtuous." They form a system.

Similarly, we must take into account the effects of emotional conditions on the church family. If certain kinds of emotionality imperil the functioning of the body's immune response, certainly they mar the healthy responses of the church family. I have learned from my experience with troubled congregations that there are generally two sets of conditions present—precipitating and contributing—and each one has one or more of these features:

Precipitating Conditions (External)

- A pastor's departure after fifteen or twenty years with the congregation
- A sequence of pastors, each averaging three to five years of service
- Trauma (major shifts in people's lives)

Contributing Conditions (Internal)

- Poorly defined boundaries in the church family (responsibility, expectation, policy, decision making)
- No clear vision
- Emotionality (more intense or more widespread)

The precipitating conditions resemble the foreign invaders in our bodies. They also stir up feelings of sorrow, helpless frustration, and pressure, which lower the responsiveness of the group. Then, if the contributing conditions exist, the capacity to respond to the precipitators is even more limited.

Some congregations remain vulnerable to the precipitators. They experience cycles of strife. The contributing conditions are never modified. They stand ready to be amused and once again reinforce the precipitating conditions. These congregations are easy to recognize. They continuously focus on external conditions to the exclusion of internal ones. They give no thought to their own immune response. They do not think systemically; they have leaders who are unresponsive, perhaps as frustrated and helpless as the rest of the organism.

SELF-DESTRUCTIVE PROTECTION

Many diseases—multiple sclerosis, rheumatoid arthritis, allergy—are the result of the immune system gone berserk. They are called autoimmune diseases. Somehow the white cells begin to attack living tissue as though it were a harmful intruder. The white cells call on the forces of expulsion. Every explosive device at their disposal is turned on simultaneously and exuberantly. When a "usually healthy reaction turns cannibalistic," physician Paul Brand notes, "a dreadful civil war" commences in the body. In the hostile presence of these defensive cells, there is overkill. More damage occurs to the host than to the invader. The defense becomes the disease. What is designed for self-protection becomes self-defeating.

Two types of hostility threaten the body physical and the body politic. *Direct* hostility is absolutely hostile. An organism contains no resources to thwart the lethal attack. Heavy dosages of radiation submit to no defensive immune reaction. Ingested, gross toxic substances poison the body. Put your hand in boiling water and damage will happen regardless of your body's defenses. In a relational context, an example of direct hostility would be an abusive father battering a helpless child.

We can also see the outcome of direct hostility in religious systems: the witch trials at Salem, Massachusetts, and the self-annihilation at Jonestown in Guyana.

The majority of survival crises that we experience with regard to health and relationship involve *indirect* hostility—"Where the response of the organism is a variable in its own survival." Two reactions are possible: a *syntonic* reaction (passive tolerance of foreign substance) or a *catatonic* reaction (excessive attack). In a catatonic attack we are actually more in danger from our own powerful reactions than from the invaders, from our own excess (extreme position) than from the antagonizer's disruption.

CATATONIC LEADERS

I have often witnessed "autoimmune disease" in troubled churches. There is fierce overreaction. These churches are in more danger from their hyper-reactionary leaders than from the contentious issues. When those who are to function as the immune cells, namely the leaders, over-react, the church is bereft of its response mechanism. The responders have become reactors. The leaders, who are positioned to mark off self from non-self, cannot differentiate because they themselves are coupled in a hostile way with the intruders.

People are overfocused on one another. Everyone's anxiety is reinforcing everyone else's. The group loses its integrity to its own reactivity—slander, blame, accusation, silent neglect, secret meetings. No one is keeping the focus on boundaries and vision. Objectivity is tossed to the winds of emotionality. The individuals designated to protect the group participate in its destruction by their own exaggerated and purposeless reactivity. Lewis Thomas has said that the arsenals our bodies possess to fight off viruses are both powerful and many. He has quipped that "we are mined" and "at the mercy of our own Pentagons." Likewise, we can diminish our relationships in excessive defense, in anxious reactivity, in extreme functioning positions. This is heightened when leaders act immaturely and automatically.

SEVEN RESPONSES

How then can leaders promote health, be our "salvation" rather than our ruin? I want to propose seven health-influencing responses. I will use a variety of stories and brief comments to illustrate each of them. The seven responses to focus on are:

- self, not others
- strength, not weakness
- process, not content
- challenge, not comfort
- integrity, not unity
- system, not symptom
- direction, not condition

So focused, leaders can be stewards of themselves and therefore stewards of the vision. Being self-defined, they can be trusted with the community's definition of itself.

THE COACH

A long-time fan of the University of North Carolina's basketball team, I once had the opportunity to watch a championship game, when North Carolina eked out a victory in the final minutes. When I was introduced to the coach afterward, I asked him, somewhat sheepishly, why he'd left a freshman in the game when he must have known that the new player would likely be fouled and forced to the free throw line. "That put a lot of pressure on a freshman," I said. Without any hesitation, the coach replied, "How else is he going to learn to handle those situations?"

"The major function of a leader," Greenleaf asserts, "is to help people to grow." Attention to weakness is anti-growth. Yet anxious people focus on weakness: "You didn't do enough." ... "I'll never get a break." In addition, anxious groups frequently have negative visions—what they don't want or what they want to get rid of or what they don't like. *Focus on strength, not weakness.*

HEY, HARRY

Working with anxious congregations, I sometimes encounter sabotage from those who are least able to regulate their anxiety. They thrive when the system's anxiety is kept alive. Somewhat perversely, they relish it. On one occasion, reviewing my report with a group of leaders, I suggested that they develop a direction with specific goals for the congregation. A man interrupted me, saying he didn't want to throw me a curve, BUT the congregation had hired an expert from California five years ago to help them do a self-study and create a corporate vision. "It didn't do us any good." He looked across the room and said, "Hey, Harry, where did we put that report?" Harry mumbled, embarrassed that he didn't know where it was located. I stayed the course. "I'm glad you knew five years ago that you needed this," I said, "and I regret that you failed to make use of it. What will be different this time so that you will be successful?"

A similar situation happened when several church members opposed contracting with me as a consultant. As far as they were concerned, my efforts would be a waste of "their" money. To prove their point, a middle-aged executive asked me, "What's your rate of success?" I told him that my rate of success was 100 percent. "My function," I added, "is to conduct and complete the process for which I contract. The rate of success for congregations working through their problems is thirty-five percent or less, depending on the degree of maturity and motivation of the leaders."

In both cases the "issue" was not really "the vision" or the "success rate." Underneath the "content," invisible emotional processes were occurring. I know that anxious people load the "issues" with emotional charge. If I, therefore, focus on the "content," I would, no doubt, enter into a contest of words and arguments. I have to remain, as best as I can, an objective, nonanxious presence, focused on my goals. Otherwise I will be pulled into the emotional glue that maintains the acute anxiety and polarization.

Focusing on the process "gives time" to the situation. Anxious groups want immediate relief and quick solutions. They panic: "This church won't survive another month." ... "Fifty people are going to leave if we don't do something soon." ... "These newcomers are taking away my church from me." If I pay attention to their "content" and rush to save them or act like an expert, I'm as anxious as they are. I reinforce their helplessness and dependency. By focusing on process, I take my time and stay goal-directed. I know that eventually we can discuss "content," but not until the reptilian regression recedes and the panic softens. *Focus on process, not content.*

HEALTH BY CHALLENGE

Leaders must learn what our physical bodies "understand"—friction is a part of life (relationship systems are inherently anxious). The body "knows" that conflict is a given. "Our own body," physician Larry Dossey writes, "contains the wisdom derived from countless challenges to its integrity." At times it fights itself, as in the autoimmune reaction. For the most part, however, the body is a masterful "conflict manager." It has learned that its health is impossible without "perturbations" (read "anxiety"). Only through threats to its well-being does the body learn to respond and to be efficient at the business of health. The essential lesson, Dossey claims, is that any health measure that does not increase our *internal wisdom* in responding to body disturbances is an inferior therapy.

Would not the same hold true for leaders in the church family? Whatever they do that does not increase the group's internal wisdom is an inferior approach. For if people are protected from threat, they become immune deficient, never to become wiser and always to be vulnerable to the newest virus.

Robert Greenleaf tells the story of John Woolman, a Quaker who lived in the mid-eighteenth century. His goal centered on abolishing the practice of enslaving people among the American Quakers. For thirty years he visited and challenged his wealthy, conservative contemporaries who used the labor of enslaved people. Nearly a century before the Civil War, the Quakers released the people they'd enslaved. Greenleaf notes that Woolman's approach was to raise questions: "What does this practice do to you as a moral person? What kind of institution are you binding over to your children?"

Questions are powerful interventions. For one thing, they point us to the imaginative capacities of the neocortex. They invite more light in; they subvert individual mind-sets or group thinking. They challenge. If we choose to be "comforters," "appeasers," or "know-it-all advisors," we are not on the side of health. Ironically, illness is the very challenge that stimulates response and promotes health. Illness and health are a system, as are anxiety and balance. In a nonthreatening, anxiety-less environment, we cannot learn how to respond. *Focus on challenge, not comfort.*

THROUGH THE WINDOW OF TRUTH

Contrary to popular notions, it is not technique, expertise, and correct formula that are needed to handle anxious relationship systems. When we work with mechanical systems, such strategies serve us well. But the mechanical world is one-sided. We repair or replace the parts that break down. Correct the cause and the effects disappear. In "living" systems, there is always information, feedback, and countermovement. The parts can react. They can sabotage and go mutinous. The parts can "blow up" in our face or "walk out" on us. The "effects" can be never-ending. We can tinker and tighten, squeeze or pound, brush or spray, and still the relationship squeaks and shakes.

Technique is a focus on the outside, on the object, on the means to get others to function as we desire. Overfocused on technique, we forfeit the opportunity to focus on how we handle ourselves. In Bill Davis' play *Mass Appeal*, we meet Father Tim Smith. He is a tinkering priest who knows how to handle the parts (members of parish). He is the epitome of the "Right Reverend Friendly." A smooth operator, Father Smith keeps the peace of his congregation. But he does not look through the window of his own soul. He is overfocused on pleasing and being nice. Confronted by a young seminarian, Mark Dolson, Father Tim comes up against his own mechanical maneuvering of his people. He even uses a mechanical image to describe how he has functioned as a priest. He confesses that he has been a "little wind-up priest doll." In a sermon, Smith admits: "Up to now, my need for your love and approval has kept me silent and inactive. This is the first time I've ever said what I wanted to you. Only now is love possible." For once, looking through the window of his own soul, he speaks the truth. He defines himself, realizing that there is no true unity if integrity is compromised. "People often want a formula, a technique, something tangible," Peter Senge declares, "that they can apply to solve the problem of structural conflict. But, in fact, being committed to the truth is far more powerful than any technique." *Focus on integrity, not unity.*

SEEING THE WHOLE

When we focus on a symptom, we are preoccupied with its cause or relief. At the same time we are not attentive to the system—the structure, patterns, and processes—behind the symptom.

Let me briefly describe how a church family moved from looking at a symptom to the system. In a period of sixteen years, the congregation had five pastors. Some blamed the church leaders, some blamed themselves, and some blamed individuals for the pastors' leaving within two or three years. Riveted to the symptom, they had to find its cause. This explains much of the blaming. What, I asked, would happen if they looked at the whole system and not the symptom alone. Motivated to turn things around, they decided that they wanted a pastor who would stay at least eight to ten years. A small group was assigned the task of asking the previous five pastors, not "Why did you leave?" but "What could you tell us that would help us keep a pastor for ten years?" Another group made the same inquiry of the membership. One of the members said she couldn't believe that change could happen by simply refocusing from "Why do pastors leave us?" to "What can we do to ensure their staying with us?"

They learned that their defeatist attitudes and demoralization curtailed their commitment. This led to the unrealistic expectation that the pastor had to motivate them and elicit their enthusiasm. The pastors felt the burden of being the only motivated persons in the relationship system. They didn't know how to change their functioning position. Incidentally, I have discovered this pattern frequently. The church family wants a pastor who will motivate them and elevate their enthusiasm. Certainly these capacities in pastoral leadership are commendable. But think for a moment how dependent this arrangement can become. Aren't people responsible for their own motivation and enthusiasm? None of us asks the plumber to motivate us so that the plumber can repair the pipes in our house. Who of us requires of the dentist that the dentist create enthusiasm on our part so that the dentist can drill our teeth or teach us effective dental care? Yet we often make one functioning position in the church family too responsible for what we individually must do for ourselves. Then, when there is a lack or enthusiasm or a failure of motivation, we look at that one position as the source of the problem. *Focus on system, not symptom.*

TODAY'S TOMORROW

Several days after Hurricane Hugo's destructive forces ravished the area around Charleston, South Carolina, I was asked to come to the city to provide support services for the clergy. Driving from the airport in Columbia toward Charleston, I listened to a number of radio programs. What most caught my attention was a brief comment made by Mayor Joseph Riley of Charleston: "We can do it!" Subsequently, I began to see these words inscribed on signs around the city. A voice had spoken out of the whirlwind. The mayor brought calm by focusing on direction, not conditions.

One of my most enjoyable consulting experiences was doing a series of leadership workshops for a church family not associated with my own denomination. They taught me much about mature cells: being responsible for themselves and responsive to others. The congregation, near its 150th anniversary, numbered about 80 people. A pastor served them for a few days each month. Five years before I made contact with them, they had decided to be a "growing" church. Located in a small Texas town, chances for growth were minimal. But they knew that the church embraced more than the mere eighty of them. They set two clear goals: 1) to raise their giving level 15 percent so that they could contribute these gifts to new congregations in other areas of the state; 2) to grow as God's people in terms of their own lives by emphasizing what for them was at the heart of their worship life, namely the Eucharist. They developed their own "Eucharistic Education Program" for all ages. A woman who was one of the "stewards of the vision" said to me: "We do a lot of remembering here. We live out our Lord's words, 'Do this in remembrance of me' in the Eucharist and 'As often as you do it unto one of the least of these, you do it unto me.' We remember the future." *Focus on direction, not condition.*

OVER AND BEYOND

Where there is little self-definition, there is a vague vision. Where there is an unclear vision, the people perish in their own anxious reactivity. They have no head and are headed nowhere. Where there is self-definition, there is a clear vision. Where there is a clear vision, there is a response to the future.

Leaders must be stewards of themselves to be stewards of the vision. They will not bend or crumble under the weight of anxiety. They press toward the goal. Leaders oversee by seeing beyond.

Being stewards of themselves, leaders can also be stewards of the relationship system. They stay connected to others and invite them to be responsible stewards of themselves and of the collective purpose. Shouldn't every church family have as much future as a past?

Chapter 10

Believing and Belonging

For each must bear his own load. . . . Bear one another's burdens, and so fulfill the law of Christ.

—Galatians 6:5,2

A Christian is a perfectly free lord of all, subject to none.
 A Christian is a perfectly dutiful servant of all, subject to all.

—Martin Luther

A RELATIONAL WORLD

Many parallels exist between "systems thinking" and the biblical record. Most notable is the interrelatedness of all things. Certainly, the biblical writers were not system thinkers in any modern sense, but they spoke of systemic forces, alive then as today. Trinitarian faith, for instance, sees all reality in relationship. God is three *separate* persons—God, the Son, and the Holy Spirit—yet *one*. Boundaries make them distinct. The historic creeds of the church indicate that the three persons of the Trinity are not fused. There is diversity in unity.

God is also separate from what is created, while not disengaged from it. In contrast to the biblical view, pantheists uphold the fusion of the Creator with the creation. Deists portray still a different God, one who is cut off from the world. According to the Scripture, God is apart from and a part of human life. God is separate from us and close to us; God is hidden and near. Thus, we stand both in awe of God's holiness or "otherness" and in confidence that God is "for us." The Israelites addressed God as Yahweh, which means "I will be who I will be." God is self-definition personified. Nevertheless, God draws close in Jesus who is called Immanuel—"God with us." For God to be God, God must function as the Holy One (*Kadosh*), that is separate and unique. Yet the Holy God is a gracious God, cutting a covenant (*berith*) with his people. "I will be your God; you will be my people." In his earthly life, Jesus faces the forces of separateness and closeness. He observes the traditions and customs of his Hebraic origin. But he also breaks the rigid boundaries of people. He talks to women in public, heals on the Sabbath, and dines with sinners—actions appropriate to his special mission of ushering in a new creation. He declares, "The father and I are one," and yet prays, "Thy will be done." He cries out, "Why have you forsaken me?"—that terrible separateness—but then places the excruciating loneliness into his Father's hands. In terms of other people, he experiences the same emotional processes. As he enters the city of Jerusalem, the people cheer him with ecstatic energy. A few days later the ecstasy turns sour, erupting into anxiety. Boldly, the disciple Peter announces that he will never forsake his master. Succumbing to his anxiety, Peter reacts and bitterly denies knowing Jesus.

On the human level the same tension of being separate from and connected to one another is alive. Indeed, we are not created to be an island unto ourself or to form a "muddy communion" in which there are two no-selves. If we are to love our neighbor as ourself, we must be as respectful of our own being as we would the other's. Paul says that we individually must bear our own load. The Greek word for "load" signifies a responsibility that we cannot delegate to another, such as a woman bearing a child or a teacher assigning grades to her students. Still, we are expected to bear the burden of others, those burdens that can be shared. In the church family, moreover, we are "individually members one of another"—separate and close. There are different *functions* that when pooled together structure and strengthen the whole.

Theologically, the overwhelming relational character of the biblical testimony is evident in sin, the aiming away from God and against the neighbor. Grace is a continuing gift to the beloved; faith is the ongoing response of trust in God's faithfulness and assent to God's presence. Righteousness is a new and right relationship with God. Christian love is being a son or daughter of the Father by functioning as a brother and sister to all the other children of God.

BROKEN BOUNDARIES

No wonder, then, that in the biblical narratives we see the twin yearnings of separateness and closeness, their extremes of cut-off and fusion, and self-definition and the lack of it, played out from generation to generation. Because of the relational character of the Bible, boundary problems—the inability to manage the tensions of self and others—are noted with frequency. Anxious reactivity, the force that leads to and permits the invasion of boundaries, filters through both testaments: from the sibling strife between Cain and Abel to the family tragedy of David's son Ammon raping his sister Tamar and Absolom's revenging Tamar's desolation in the annihilation of his brother Ammon; from the jealousy aroused when a couple of disciples of Jesus seek favored positions in the Kingdom to come to the estrangement between the apostle Paul and a member of the Christian community—"Alexander the coppersmith did me great harm."

The interrelatedness of life means that we will always deal with emotional processes. As levels of anxiety increase, we become more instinctual. It's a matter of survival. Power struggles, jealousies, betrayals, splits, and other forms of broken boundaries ensue. And what was operative in the biblical world is at work today. The stories are mirrors, reflections of our own world. Church families, therefore, subject to emotional processes, will have their Cains, Davids, and Alexanders. But too many church families live with the idealized notion that they are perpetual havens of love and peace. They are oblivious to the reality of normal emotional processes. Thus, when boundaries are violated by rumors, gossip, and secret alliances, the violations are passively tolerated or ignored. Many fear that if the forces are openly confronted, feelings will be hurt, members will be lost, and friendships will be shattered. As a result, criticizers and attackers, privilege seekers and power brokers, the least motivated and most recalcitrant are allowed to roam at will. Like cancer cells, they go where they don't belong, and no one tells them they can't stay there or don't belong there. Their intrusion is permitted and enabled. Instead of attending to the regulation of ourselves, courageous responses, and commitment to beliefs and purpose, we become organized around our anxiety, which drains our energies and resources.

RESPONSE AND RECOVERY

"System theory provides no magical answers," Murray Bowen remarks, "but it does provide a different way of conceptualizing human problems." We learn that in relationship we do not act completely on our own "steam." Nor do we always express ourselves, simply because of our "nature." Environment is always an influence. "It is the context," Gregory Bateson contends, "that fixes meaning." We are constantly influencing the behaviors of others and likewise being influenced by them. Looking at what takes place *between* people, we observe the reciprocal influences and the mutual reinforcement of functioning positions. This does not mean that there is no sense of individual responsibility. If anything, systems thinking elevates the need to be responsible. Individually, we decide who will or will not be allowed in our personal space, what we will stand for and what will not be tolerated, and how far or close the sphere of influence will be negotiated. Being responsible, for example, we set our own limits, not someone else's. We regulate our own anxiety rather than assigning it to others in the form of criticism or fault-finding. We look at how we can change ourselves instead of how we can force or manipulate others to make changes in themselves. This is more than psychology. It goes to the very core of creation theology, that we are created to be responsible creatures. One of the words that church has used to distinguish responsible living is "stewardship." A steward is a manager of what is given. Our primary responsibility is the management of our own life and the relationships we form—anxiety and all.

A number of studies have highlighted the significance of the stewardship of the self. It is a key factor in the promotion of mental and physical well-being. Researcher Pettingale and others have studied the effect of psychological response to early breast cancer and its relation to survival. Ten years after the onset of the disease, women who responded with helplessness or passivity had a lower rate of survival than those who responded with a fighting spirit. The stewards of themselves had a survival rate three times that of those who gave up self-management. Further, Professor David Spiegel conducted a study of similar patients, discovering that those with breast cancer who had joined with other women in group psychotherapy lived twice as long as those who did not. Being responsive to others through genuine consolation and conversation is healing medicine. Physician James J. Lynch found the same to be true relative to the functioning of the heart. He calls companionship one of the best forms of life insurance.

On the negative side, Dutch cardiologist A. J. Dunning discusses extremes in human behavior and their effect on health. One extreme was the strange ailment that appeared after World War I called "soldier's heart." Anxiety, which aggravates many conditions of illness, was intense in the front trenches of the war. Soldiers who suppressed it paid the price in bodily fatigue, heart palpitations, shortness of breath, and inability to exert effort. Lack of response to their anxiety and lack of response to others about the anxiety found an outlet in illness. More recently, the research of psychology professor James W. Pennebaker has uncovered the same phenomenon. The capacity to confide in others has a healing power, and the incapacity diminishes health. Inhibition, secrets, unspoken trauma, mental blocking of pain, mindless distraction—all enable the disease process. What are automatic processes, intended for survival for the moment, become habits. Yet ultimately they do not serve the healing process and enhance survival. Without movement from reaction to response, there is no wholeness.

Looking through more than 300 genograms which I have constructed with clients in psychotherapy, I see the same "evidence" of life's diminishment. The multi-generational diagrams illustrate that those families who deny and do not work through pain have outlets for it in symptoms—alcohol abuse, sexual trauma, mental illness, physical attack, suicide, emotional cutoff, excessive dependency, hostile coupling of family members, and many other forms of "acting out" the emotional pain. The family system suppresses, denies, or ignores its anxiety, which simply goes underground and surfaces in one or more of the family members. But family members rivet attention on the symptomatic member, missing what generates anxiety in the first place and how it is mutually maintained over time, even through generations.

If relational processes are similar to cellular processes, no relationship system can sustain or restore its health without positive response: focus of its energy in goal-directed activity; awareness; self-management; sense of meaning, thoughtfulness, mutual exchange; and dialogue. In their absence the natural healing processes of the system decline. Indeed, strong reactivity in harsh circumstances is *normal*. It is not pain translated into reactive positions that is the ultimate danger. Rather, if what is intended to be immediate becomes longstanding, a pattern develops, stubborn in its resistance to change. Strong anxiety will override good sense, commitment to beliefs, clarity, direction, creativity, and response. The system locks itself into its own automatic and defensive processes. In essence, the system chooses immediate security over learning, harmony over transformation, passivity and helplessness over stewardship, disease over change, the elimination of symptoms over altering the reactive processes. It does not trust what is difficult.

"Anxiety in its nakedness," theologian Paul Tillich declared, "is always the anxiety of ultimate non-being." The stakes are high—survival. Hence we use each other to defend the preservation of self. We act like children who, lacking the capacity to define self to others, defend self *against* others or surrender self *to* others. In adult stewardship, however, we see what is *happening* as a challenge; we see that the very threat of non-being can be the occasion of strengthening being: defining self and staying in touch with others.

FORGIVENESS

Sustained and strong anxiety tests the church family at the deepest point of its life together—the responses of faith and love. Moreover, most biblical spirituality is born in the wilderness and Gethsemane, when Absalom is killed and Gomer is unfaithful, at the edge of Nineveh and Samaria. These are the ripe moments and places for launching into growth and new dimensions of thought, relation, and trust. Anxiety puts our response capacities, especially faith and love, to a rigorous test.

Nowhere is the tension more challenging than in the sphere of who we are and what we are about as a Christian community—forgiveness. For forgiveness always occurs in a context of emotional processes. When we are severely anxious, therefore more automatic and reactive, we are less clear and focused, less calm and thoughtful, less directed and decisive. If offended, we may distance. Avoidance behaviors are common in conflict. In return for the resumption of our participation, we set conditions on others. The offender must be expunged, bow to our position, or pay a ransom. This, though, is bargaining, not forgiving. In conditional love there is no letting go or release. Further, we act as if the only way we can have a "self" is "over against" the offender and not from within ourselves.

If offended, we may revert to the other extreme. We cover the offense lightly, "Let bygones be bygones." We deny our own hurt to obtain the approval we need from others or to secure the harmony the group demands. We rush into congeniality and congeal. The "self" is dissolved in boundarylessness. But love without shape or form will perpetuate injustice. Instead of release, "bleeding hearts" merely reinforce transgression (the crossing of boundaries). Forgiveness does not mean putting up with fools. It does not mean protecting those who think the way we think regardless of how deceitful or mean-spirited they act. Forgiveness is not "letting off the hook" because after all the "bum" must have some redeeming qualities. God works with redeeming love, not on the basis of human qualities.

We forgive to restore a relationship, not to relieve our own anxiety. If we make demands about how others should function a condition for the resumption of our participation in or return to the group, we are not interested in extending forgiveness. If we comply with group pressure for the sake of peace and tranquility, we are not interested in forgiveness. Indeed, Jesus prayed to his Father to forgive his offenders. But he didn't ask for their pardon to diminish his own anxiety or theirs. He saw their mindlessness—"for they know not what they do."

Forgiveness requires some capacity to "stand back"—to be self-regulated and objective. Anxiety, rooted in the naked threat of non-being, incites the feeling process that is linked to the automatic side of life: survival and self-preservation. Thus, thinking and seeing clearly always lose in high-density anxiety. This does not mean that feelings are harmful and thoughts are beneficial. Rather, thinking does not eliminate feeling processes. It brings them to awareness, to the point where we can be responsible for them. When we "rationalize" our feelings—deny, dissociate, or justify them—we are not being objective. Actually, we are controlled by our anxiety, merely using the Thinking Cap to reduce threat and escape responsibility.

We need, therefore, to see forgiveness more as a process than an event, a discovery than a fiat. It takes time to let emotional heat cool down and to move from survival to "sober judgment." God's forgiveness is a free gift. There are no "strings attached"—that is, "you must change" (so I can feel less anxious) or "I must give up self" (so everyone else feels less anxious). God's forgiveness cannot be fiddled with, modified, or altered. It is irreversible. It is *there*. Human forgiveness is slower and more erratic. It is always entangled in our creature anxiety. But it's not impossible. Forgiven, we are secure in our relationship with God. Nothing will separate us from the love of God in Christ Jesus. Our ultimate hope is not in reptilian processes but in a resurrected Lord. So centered, we can extend forgiveness to others. If we possess the future, we need not be anxious in every threatening moment.

WHAT IS SOWN IS REAPED

As part of the process of working with emotionally charged church families, I routinely ask what biblical words or stories come to mind with regard to their anxious situation. Also, I inquire about how they understand what is happening theologically or what "spiritual" work is needed to be done. The responses are weak. Many moralize about "right and wrong." Others use words like "reconciliation, forgiveness, and love" but without much depth to their comments. Far too many avoid the question altogether and resort to cliches such as "power struggle," "the alligators are biting," "poor chemistry," and "a terrible mess." If my experience is an accurate sample, many church families have little capacity to *define* themselves in terms of their own Christian faith. They fail to bring to their emotional processes that which would help them recognize why they have come together, how they can define themselves to what is happening in the moment, and where they need to proceed in the future. They do not utilize their symbols, ceremonies, and stories as means to *differentiate* themselves from other human associations. They claim they are "holy" (set apart for God's purposes) but function as if they are common entities. Church families are not different in their experience of emotional processes but one might expect a difference in how they respond to them. Such a response would be predicated on the community's beliefs. Too often congregations trade their beliefs for safety in numbers, their convictions for immediate solutions, and their values for survival.

"We fritter away our destiny," theologian Harvey Cox has said, "by letting some snake tell us what to do." The first relationship system is but a mirror of all systems. And church families can fritter away their destinies by letting their own reptilian processes tell them what to do.

Those who do move toward their destinies do so through *metanoia*, a changing of mind, an imaginative response, an acceptance of anxiety's challenge to change and grow.

"So then, as we have opportunity, let us do good to all . . . especially to those who are of the household of faith" (Galatians 6:10).

Appendix A
Systems and Implementing Change

"For me, it is so simple," Brandon remarked, "that any reasonable person would do the same." Brandon was referring to a protocol set up to avoid accidents at his company. Nonetheless, supervisors decided to waive the requirements and speed up the manufacturing process. Irritated Brandon tried to rally other employees to object to the degrading of safety rules. In order to mute his complaints, he was soon sent to a less visible position. Brandon's suggestion to incorporate safety in a process to ensure less chance of physical harm made sense but slowed the process of production. It was rational and tested. But company profits held sway over engineered safety.

Ted and Cora are teachers at a grade school with mostly Latino students. Both listened carefully to their students' fears—bullying, especially for recruitment by gang members, and the threat of abduction. Ted and Cora spoke to the administration and said it was crucial that they organize a program of safety for the children. The school social worker, Angelina, supported the effort, and Father Damascus from the local Roman Catholic Church promised the assistance of the parish. Most of the children walked to school and back and were often accosted. About half of them had parents or relatives who were legal residents. Some were "dreamers"; some lived with relatives, and others lived with adults who were undocumented. Maria's parents had been deported, and she lived with her aunt who worked at a low-paying job. To make ends meet for her aunt and her two children, Maria, at the age of thirteen, turned to prostitution. Angelina had been working intently with Maria to get her out of this dangerous situation, but before she was able to help her, Angelina was shot and killed. Angelina, a sturdy, stoic person herself, went to the administration in tears. She pleaded for a school safety program. Ted and Cora excoriated the principal for her delay and procrastination. It took the brutal murder of Maria for the system to finally act.

Hakim, never shy about being progressive in his denomination's affairs, faulted the leadership for offering a health plan for workers that met only minimum medical needs. In turn, the officials defended themselves, saying that they had to tighten benefits in order to balance income and expenditures. Seeking its own solution, Hakim's church installed a hotline for those in need of treatment, via telemedicine. Some members volunteered to bring food and run errands for the indigent. Through his determination and example, he eventually persuaded the national office to seek out and reinstate some medical benefits for the most needy.

Any one of these systems could be described by organizational expert William Deming's observation: "Your system is perfectly designed for the results you are getting." If the results are inadequate, the system needs to change.

Corpus Christi Episcopal Church discovered that people who returned from mission trips had a renewed spirit that led to personal changes. From this observation, the rector saw an opportunity to teach "mission." The congregation would encourage hands-on efforts of loving one's neighbor. Formerly, the church fulfilled its mission objectives with cash or durable goods. Now, people were encouraged to be part of a tutoring program, work the food bank, and assist senior citizens. It was a redesign. Alongside the discovery of concrete, direct service as a teaching tool, they realized that change was resisted less if it were connected to the mission.

We know that the Christian Church in America has plunged into decline. Someone said that "when we don't get what we want, we want what we get." We become satisfied no matter what the results may be. I won't make friends saying the following, but as an observer of the church, the situation is too often rationalized with sayings such as "the church has always had dry periods" or "we need to ask not what we can do but what God is doing." This puts history on one's side and triangles God in the dilemma. But we are imaginative creatures. I wonder if God is saying, "What can you imagine? How can you put a new system in place?"

Appendix B

Imagining the Future Church

With so much "up in the air" and encased in uncertainty, writing about the future of anything is an exercise of futility, maybe hubris. For sure, I am not prescient in any measure beyond the normal. I am not a clairvoyant, a stargazer, forecaster, or a thinker known for thinking outside the box, but still, I want to emphasize the power of imagination. It can go awry or to extremes, yet imagination is a mental gift bestowed on humans alone. Without it, we would be riveted to routine and bored with repeated patterns. Imagination is part of God's design. We are to use it to the best of our ability and for the benefit of others. The theology of creation invites us to be imaginatively wise. We often associate creation with earth, water, and air, the external environment, at the loss of personal and interpersonal gifts like imagination and cooperation. That we can exercise this mental ability in perverse or bizarre ways does not take away from the gift itself. In human hands and thoughts, anything can be distorted. We do not cease being lovers because even the wonderful gift of love can be misused. Being formed in the image of God the Creator is the first indication that the creative urge depends on the capacity to imagine. "Without imagination," Gloria Steinem declared, "we lose the excitement of possibilities." We need probably more now than ever, the imagination of a future that does not exist.

Concerning the church system in the United States, my assumption is that it has kept imagination in "protective custody," fearing it might go out of control, as it has in the past with heresies, false clams, distorted promises, and nefarious behaviors. Letting imagination be freewheeling, you rattle or shatter standards and traditional practices. Imagination is the friend of change, and that in itself could be the reason for keeping it in protective custody.

Throughout his public ministry, Jesus taught the same lesson: "Metanoia! The kingdom of God is at hand." Unfortunately, St. Jerome translated the word "metanoia" from Greek to Latin and used a Latin word associated with "penance." Jesus is saying more than have remorse or regret as the Latin word would indicate. Nowhere in the literature of the first century is the word "metanoia" used for sorrow or regret. "Meta" means "beyond." There is a sense of spaciousness. Metaphysics means "beyond the material world." "Noia" derives from "nous" (mind). What he meant was so profound that Jesus had to use the simple means to convey what he meant—parables. He appealed to the imagination.

My view is that the gift of imagination can energize the church system and contribute to the common good in a complex world. For a faith-based community that confesses in one of the creeds that they "look for the life of the world to come" to be cautious about imagination is facetious. Metanoia is always on the table. Cutting eschatology in half by obsessing on the present and neglecting the "not yet" of God's promises is a sign of little faith. Daily, the church prays, "Thy kingdom come on earth as in heaven." The church invented the "O antiphons" of Advent, acknowledging its hope—"Come, Lord Jesus."

Albert Einstein said imagination allows you to circle the globe. You are put into motion. And the poet Emily Dickinson is a superb guide: "Not knowing when the dawn will appear, I open all the doors." At a time when our world is not much different from the infant's, "a big blooming, buzzing confusion," we need to see what is possible. The slow fuse of the possible is the imagination.

The vast majority of clergy in the United States have been trained to be geographers. They know the map and territory, the lay of the land. They know the rubrics of worship and the hermeneutical tools needed for interpretation. They are homileticians, exegetes, pastors, evangelists, administrators, and systematicians—generalists. They were taught by other geographers, some good noes too. Very few of our instructors were explorers; very few served as the "man in the arena." Though seminaries advertise offerings of transformative leadership, it's doubtful that their graduates are tinkerers. They turn into geographers.

In the last month, I have had three clergies tell me that despite the national trend of lower numbers in membership and worship attendance, they still have to fight off self-doubt and self-blame. These trained geographers question their relevance. To explore the terrain, the waterways, and the topography of a changing world is not consonant with their embedded image of ministry. Anyway, many of the congregations they serve prefer to have a geographer in place.

The predominance of what has been changing is external, conditional, and cultural. Surely, the church's refusal or hesitancy to release imagination from protective custody is a contributor. The church does not ordain specifically, but Metanoia is always on the table. Change is constant.

We seldom welcome explorers in the ranks of laity either. When they join the church we want to be sure they are geographers. We ask for confirmation of what they believe. They are not asked if they would be explorers, disciples, learners. The church likes compliers, consumers, those who have the same theological chromosomes. They champion explorers like Calvin, Luther, Schweitzer, Bonhoeffer, and Mandella, so long as they remain in the history books.

What will it take to have an Imaginative Reformation? Thankfully, I have had a chance to see glimpses of exploration in my work. I hope it elicits a conversation about rivers, deserts, and mountains.

Bibliography

Bonhoeffer, Dietrich. *Life Together.* San Francisco: HarperCollins, 1954.

Bowen, Murray. *Family Therapy in Clinical Practice.* Northvale, NJ: Jason Aronson, 1985.

Brand, Paul and Philip Yancey. *Fearfully and Wonderfully Made.* Grand Rapids, MI: Zondervan, 1987.

Buechner, Frederick. *Telling Secrets.* San Francisco: HarperCollins, 1991.

Davis, Bill C. *Mass Appeal.* New York: Avon Books, 1981.

Dossey, Larry. *Meaning and Medicine.* New York: Bantam Books, 1991.

Friedman, Edwin H. *Generation to Generation: Family Process in Church and Synagogue.* New York: The Guilford Press, 1985.

Gasset, Ortega. *Man and Crisis.* New York: W. W. Norton and Company, 1958.

Greenleaf, Robert K. *Servant Leadership.* New York: Paulist Press, 1977.

Hoffman, Lynn. *Foundations of Family Therapy.* New York: Basic Books, 1981.

Huxley, Aldous. *The Devils of Loudon.* New York: Carroll and Graf, 1986.

Kopp, Sheldon. *An End to Innocence: Facing Life Without Illusions.* New York: Bantam Books, 1978.

————. *This Side of Tragedy: Psychotherapy as Theater.* Palo Alto, CA: Science and Behavior Books, 1977.

Nisbet, Robert. *Social Change.* New York: Harper and Row, 1973.

Papero, Daniel V. *Bowen Family Systems Theory.* Boston: Allyn and Bacon, 1990.

Rilke, Rainer Maria. *Letters to a Young Poet.* New York: Vintage Books, 1986.

Ripley, Amanda. *The Unthinkable: Who Survives Disaster and Why.* n.p.: Harmony, 2009.

Senge, Peter M. *The Fifth Discipline: The Art and Practice of the Learning Organization*. New York: Doubleday Currency, 1990.

Thomas, Lewis. *The Lives of a Cell*. New York: The Viking Press, 1974.

———. *The Medusa and the Snail*. New York: Bantam Books, 1980.

Tillich, Paul. *The Courage to Be*. New Haven, CT: Yale University Press, 1952.

Index

Page references for diagrams, illustrations, and tables are italicized.

Aaron (biblical priest), 66
Abraham (biblical patriarch), *37*, 38, 39, *39*
accomplices, 60
acute anxiety, 23, 24, 48–49
Adam (biblical figure), 30, 50, *50*
agency, 44–45
alcohol and immune system, 105
animals, social, 91–92
anorexia nervosa, 14
anxiety: acute, 23, 24, 48–49; as binding, 59–61; case study, 76–79, *77*, *78*, *79*; chronic, 23–26, 48; in the church, as given, 2–3; energy and, 42; faith and, 2; flow of, *77*, 77–79, *78*, *79*; focus of, 17; habitual, 23–24, 25–26, 48; negative outcomes of, 21–23; in relationships, 17–18; reptilian brain and, 42; about separateness and closeness, 32–33, 34; situational, 23, 24, 48–49; source of, 76–77; as term, 18; as trap, 62–63; triggers, 17; vicious circle of, *26*, 26–27, *27*. *See also*
anxiety and reactivity; triune brain
anxiety and reactivity: about, 45–46; burden shifting, 48–54; circle, tightening of, 47–48; perspective, narrow, 46–47; triangling, 49–53, *50*, *51*, *53*
atomic holocaust, 44, 45
Augsburger, David, 49–50
autoimmune diseases, 107
Automatic Pilot, 18, 19, *19*, 20–21, 25–26, 42

balance, restoring, 101
Bateson, Gregory, 9, 118
benign neglect, 82
Bible: anxiety, 27–28; burden shifting, 50, *50*; demons, naming, 64–65; family structure/ functioning, *37*, 37–39, *39*; Genesis creation story, 29–30; Gerasene demoniac, 64–64; golden calf story, 66; interrelatedness of all things, 115–16; metaphors, 1; perception,

133

distorted, 46–47; secrecy, 90;
separateness and closeness,
family example, *37*, 37–39, *39*;
system theory, parallels with,
115–16; triangling, 50, *50*
biological system, 10
Black Death, 43–44, 45
blame, 55, 112–13
body of Christ metaphor, 57–58,
80–81
Bonhoeffer, Dietrich, 1–2
boundaries, broken, 117–18
Bowen, Murray, 14, 32, 118. *See
also* self-differentiation
brain. *See* triune brain
Brand, Paul, 63, 80–81, 107
breast cancer patients, 118–19
Bridgebuilder facilitators, vii
Buechner, Frederick, 14
burden shifting: about, 48–49; in Bible,
50, *50*; church families, *50*, 50–52,
51, *53*, 53–54; targets, prime, 52;
triangling, 49–53, *50*, *51*, *53*

Cana wedding feast, 84–85
cancer cells, 80, 81, 117. *See also*
breast cancer patients
Cannon, Walter B., 10
care, 58, 59, 61
caretaking, exaggerated, 100
case studies: anxiety, 76–79, *77*,
78, *79*; Community Church, 96,
97, *97*, 99; emotional processes,
71–72; First Church, 54–56, *55*;
maturity, 96–99, *97*; problem,
redefining, 54–56, *55*; reactivity
to response, moving from, 86–
88, 89, 91; self-differentiation,
86–88, 89, 91; triangling, 79, *80*;
Trinity Church, 86–88, 89, 91;
Unity Church, 96–99, *97*. *See
also* Transfiguration Church case
study

catatonic reaction, 108
cells: cancer, 80, 81, 117; fusion of,
104–5; mature, 114
cerebral hemispheres, 19, *19*, 20, 21
challenge, focus on, 110–11
change, implementing, 125–26. *See
also* stability and change
Charleston, South Carolina, 113–14
child development, 30–31
children, resiliency in, 40
chosen child role, 38
chronic anxiety, 23–24, 25–26, 48
church: anxiety in the, 2–3; body
of Christ metaphor for, 57–58;
future, imagining, 127–29; growth
of, 114; as term, 57
church families: as concept, 3–4;
processes, 40–42; reactivity to
response, moving from, 86–88,
89, 91; separateness and
closeness, 40–42; triangling in,
50, 50–52, *51*, *53*, 53–54
Churchill, Winston, 106
circle, tightening of, 47–48
circles of influence: about, 8–9;
patterned/repeated, 10–12
clarity and compassion, 57–67;
anxiety, as binding, 59–61;
anxiety, as trap, 62–63; body
of Christ metaphor, 57–58;
demons, naming, 64–65; health as
response, 63–64; pain tolerance,
61–62, *62*; purpose bonding,
65–67; romantic love, 58–59
closeness. *See* separateness and
closeness
clutching others (functioning
position), 34, *35*
comfort, focus on, 110–11
Community Church case study, 96,
97, *97*, 99
compassion. *See* clarity and
compassion

complementary relationships, 13, 61–62
condition, focus on, 113–14
conflict, 54–56, *55*, 110–11
conspiracy, 44
content, focus on, 109–10
contrary relationships, 13
contributing conditions, 107
convictions, 90–91
Copernicus's theory, 85
Corinth, chaos at, 90
Corinthians, 27
Corpus Christi Episcopal Church, 126
Council of Jerusalem, 90
COVID-19 pandemic, 45
Cox, Harvey, 122
creation, Genesis story of, 29–30
criticism, 89
crowd delirium, 48
culture shock, 11
Cupid, 58
cutting off (functioning position), 34, *35*

Davis, Bill, 112
defining self (functioning position), 34, *34*, *35*
Deming, William, 126
demons, naming, 64–65
The Devils of London (Huxley), 47–48
Dickinson, Emily, 128
direct hostility, 107–8
direction, focus on, 113–14
disasters, 43–44, 45
disciples, 84
disease, 10, 80–81, 82, 107
disruptions, major, 49
A Distant Mirror (Tuchman), 43–44
Dossey, Larry, 111
Dunning, A. J., 119

Eddington, Arthur, 59
Einstein, Albert, 128

emotional fusion, 32, 38, 59
emotional processes: case studies, 71–72; in families, *37*, 37–38, *39*; harmful, 80–82; interrelatedness of life and, 117–18; as invisible, 3
energy, directing, 42
enslaved people, 111
Esau (biblical figure), *37*, 38, 39, *39*
Eve (biblical figure), 50, *50*
external conditions, 106, 107

faith, 2
families: emotional processes, *37*, 37–38, *39*; genograms, 37, *37*, *39*, 119; restorative powers of, 39–40; separateness and closeness, influence on, 36–40, *37*, *39*. *See also* church families
family hero role, 38
First Church case study, 54–56, *55*
flagellants, 44
forgiveness, 120–22
friction, 54–56, *55*, 110–11
Friedman, Edwin: disease processes and emotional processes, 80; *Generation to Generation*, xi; golden calf story, 66; immaturity, 60; leadership, 82, 103–4; reptilian regression, 21; shark story, 99–100; stressors, 45
functioning positions: clutching others, 34, *35*; cutting off, 34, *35*; defining self, 34, *34*, *35*; separateness and closeness, 32–33, *33*, 34, *34*, *35*; touching others, 34, *34*, *35*
future church, imagining, 127–29

Galileo, 85
Gasset, Ortega, 32
Generation to Generation (Friedman), xi
Genesis creation story, 29–30

genograms, 37, *37*, *39*, 119
Gerasene demoniac, 64–64
God, nature of, 115–16
goggizo, as term, 89
golden calf, 66
gossip, 50
grace, 2
gravity, 8–9
Great Mortality, 43–44, 45
Greenleaf, Robert, 103, 109, 111
grief, 40–41

habitual anxiety, 23–24, 25–26, 48
health, 10, 63–64
Healthy Congregations project, vii
Hellenists, 27
herd-poison, 47–48
Hezekiah (King of Judah), 46–47
Hiroshima atomic explosion, 44, 45
Hoffman, Lynn, 9
homeostasis, 10, 56
hostility, 60–61, 107–8
House of Emotion, 18–19, *19*, 19–21
human problems, conceptualizing, 118
Hurricane Hugo, 113–14
Huxley, Aldous, 47–48
hypersensitivity, 63, 64
hysteria, mass, in Ursuline convent, 47

ideals, 1
identified problem, 51
illness, 10, 80–81, 82, 107
imagination, 127–29
immaturity, 95–96, *96. See also*
    maturity
immune system, 104–6, 107
Indianapolis (USS Cruiser), 99–100
indirect hostility, 108
integrity, focus on, 111–12
internal conditions, 107

internal wisdom, 111
interrelatedness, 115–16, 117–18
Isaac (biblical patriarch), *37*, 38, 39, *39*
Israelites, 27–28, 116

Jacob (biblical patriarch), *37*, 38, 39, *39*
Jesus: Cana wedding feast, 84–85;
    forgiveness, 121; imagination,
    appealing to, 128; self-giving, 84;
    separateness and closeness, 116;
    wilderness temptations, 50
Jews, as scapegoats during Great
    Mortality, 44
Job (biblical figure), 46
Joseph (son of Jacob, biblical figure),
    37, 38, 39, *39*

Laban (biblical figure), 38, 39
Lear, Norman, 47
learn, capacity to, 44–45
"The Lesson," 22–23
levity, 9
Lewin, Kurt, 91
life, stewardship of, xii
life crises, 49
Lifton, Robert Jay, 44
limbic system, 18–19, *19*, 19–21
liquor and immune system, 105
living world *versus* physical world, 9
locusts, 91–92
Loudon, Ursuline convent in, 47
love, romantic, 58–59
Luther, Martin, 82
lymphocytes, 105, 106, 107
Lynch, James J., 119

MacLean, Paul, 18. *See also* triune
    brain
mammalian brain, 18–19, *19*, 19–21
Mass Appeal (Davis), 112

mass hysteria in Ursuline convent, 47
Matthean sayings, 90
mature cells, 114
maturity: about, 93–94; balance,
    restoring, 101; case studies, 96–
    99, *97*; immaturity *versus*, 95–96,
    96; stressors and, *94*, 94–95, *95*
mechanical systems, 111–12
medical benefits for needy, 126
Mencken, Henry, 58
metanoia, 128, 129
metaphors, 1, 57–58, 80–81
Minuchin, Salvador, 31
mission, teaching, 126
Moses (biblical leader), 27–28, 66
mutuality, 58, 59, 60–61, 66

Nagasaki atomic explosion, 44, 45
Native Americans, 105
neglect, benign, 82
neocortex, 19, *19*, 20, 21

others, focus on, 109
overfocus, 88–89, 108

pain, 61–62, *62*, 100
parent-child relationships, 12–13
parts: influence on each other, 8–9;
    interrelatedness of, 7–8; whole,
    organization of, 12–13
pastors: in conflict with
    congregation, 54–56, *55*; in
    crisis, 52; grief surrounding loss
    of endeared, 40–41; problem,
    redefining, 54–56, *55*; as
    triangling targets, 52; turnover in,
    112–13. *See also* Transfiguration
    Church case study
Pennebaker, James W., 119
perception, distorted, 46–47
perspective, narrow, 46–47
Peter, the Apostle, Saint, 116

physical world *versus* living world, 9
Piaget, Jean, 8
plague, 43–44, 45
political system, 10
precipitating conditions, 106, 107
problems: human, conceptualizing,
    118; identified, 51; redefining,
    54–56, *55*
process, focus on, 109–10
prodigal son, parable of, 24–25
prophets, 47, 83–84. *See also* self-
    differentiation
protection, self-destructive, 107–8
purpose, 44–45
purpose bonding, 65–67
pursuit behavior, 88–89

Quakers, 111
questions, as powerful interventions,
    111

Rachel (biblical matriarch), *37*, 38,
    39
reactivity. *See* anxiety and reactivity
reactors, 60, 61, 65–66, 108
reaping what's sown, 122–23
Rebekah (biblical matriarch), *37*,
    38, *39*
regression, reptilian, 21–23
relationships: anxiety in, 17–18;
    complementary, 13, 61–62;
    contrary, 13; parent-child, 12–13
relationship system, stewardship of,
    114
reptilian brain, 18, 19, *19*, 20–21,
    25–26, 42
reptilian regression, 21–23
rescue, 88
resiliency, 40
responses: about, 108–9; challenge
    versus comfort, 110–11; direction
    versus condition, 113–14; health

as, 63–64; integrity *versus* unity,
111–12; process *versus* content,
109–10; recovery and, 118–20;
self *versus* others, 109; strength
versus weakness, 109; system
versus symptom, 112–13
restorative powers of families, 39–40
Riley, Joseph, 113–14
Rilke, Rainer Maria, 42
Ripley, Amanda, 44–45
romantic love, 58–59

safety programs, 125–26
Salem (Massachusetts) witch trials,
85, 108
sanitary conditions during Great
Mortality, 44
Sarah (biblical matriarch), *37*, 38, *39*
scapegoats, sin-bearing, 43–44
Schaef, Anne Wilson, 60
secrecy, 89–90
self: focus on, 109; stewardship of,
104, 109, 114, 118–19; as term,
15
self-destructive protection, 107–8
self-differentiation: about, 14–15,
32, 66; case study, 86–88, 89, 91;
reactions to, 84–85; stewardship
of life and, xii; undifferentiation
versus, 91–92, *92*; vision
safeguards and, 103–4
Selye, Hans, 72–73
Senge, Peter, 103
sentimental care, 59, 61
sentimentalism, 59–60, 61, 65–66
separateness and closeness: about,
13–14; anxiety about, 32–33, 34;
biblical family example, *37*, 37–
39, *39*; child development and,
30–31; church family processes,
40–42; as driving forces, 31–32;
family influence on, 36–40, *37*,

39; functioning positions, 32–33,
33, 34, *34*, *35*; Genesis creation
story, 29–30; Jesus, 116; self-
differentiation and, 14–15, 32
shark story, 99–100
similar relationships, 13
situational anxiety, 23, 24, 48–49
slavery, 111
social conditions and immune
function, 106
soft care, 59, 61
"soldier's heart," 119
Spiegel, David, 118–19
stability and change: about, 12;
anxiety and reactivity, 45–54;
burden shifting, 48–54; circle,
tightening of, 47–48; disasters,
43–44; perspective, narrow, 46–
47; problem, redefining, 54–56,
55; triangling, 49–53, *50*, *51*, *53*
Steinem, Gloria, 127
stewardship: about, 118, 120; of life,
xii; of relationship system, 114;
of self, 104, 109, 114, 118–19; of
vision, 103–4, 109, 114
stories, 64
straight-line thinking, 8, 9, *9*
strength, focus on, 109
stressors, *94*, 94–95, *95*
symptom, focus on, 112–13
syntonic reaction, 108
system: biological, 10; defined, 7,
8; focus on, 112–13; immune,
104–6, 107; implementing change
and, 125–26; limbic, 18–19, *19*,
19–21; relationship, 114; water as
part of, 9
system theory: biblical record,
parallels with, 115–16; circles
of influence, 8–9; circles of
influence, patterned/repeated,
10–12; human problems,

conceptualizing, 118; straight-line thinking *versus*, 8, 9, *9*; whole, 7–8, 12–13. *See also* separateness and closeness; stability and change

Tavris, Carol, 23
Thinking Cap, 19, *19*, 20, 21
Thomas, Lewis, 63, 80, 81, 91–92, 104–5, 108
Thomas Aquinas, Saint, 2
"three advantages" in crisis and recovery, 44–45
Tillich, Paul, 120
touching others (functioning position), 34, *34*, *35*
Transfiguration Church case study: about, 73–74; anxiety, flow of, *77*, 77–79, *78*, *79*; anxiety, source of, 76–77; historical conditions, 74, *74*; structure and function, 75, *75*; triangles, 79, *80*
triangling: about, 49–50; in Bible, 50, *50*; case study, 79, *80*; in church family, *50*, 50–52, *51*, *53*, 53–54; targets, prime, 52
Trinity, viii, 115
Trinity Church case study, 86–88, 89, 91
triune brain: about, 18–19, *19*; mammalian brain, 18–19, *19*, 19–21; neocortex, 19, *19*, 20, 21;

reptilian brain, 18, 19, *19*, 20–21, 25–26, 42
Tuchman, Barbara, 43–44

undifferentiation, 91–92, *92*. *See also* self-differentiation
unity, focus on, 111–12
Unity Church case study, 96–99, *97*
University of North Carolina basketball team, 109
unresponsiveness, 106–7
The Unthinkable (Ripley), 44–45
Ursuline convent, 47
USS Cruiser *Indianapolis*, 99–100

vicious circle of anxiety, *26*, 26–27, *27*
vision, 103–4, 109, 114

water as part of system, 9
weakness, focus on, 109
Weil, Simone, 24
white cells, 105, 106, 107
whole, in system theory, 7–8, 12–13
wilderness temptations of Jesus, 50
willfulness, 24
wisdom, internal, 111
witch trials of Salem, Massachusetts, 85, 108
Wolin, Steve, 39–40
Woolman, John, 111

About the Author

Peter L. Steinke was an internationally recognized leadership consultant who served as a parish pastor, therapist, director of a counseling center, educator, and founder of Healthy Congregations. He is the author of several books, including *Uproar: Calm Leadership in Anxious Times* and *Teaching Fish to Walk: Church Systems and Adaptive Challenge*.

Made in United States
Orlando, FL
10 December 2021

11440830R00087

"There is no better guide through the invisible processes and systems that shape our lives together in church than Peter L. Steinke. Our leading authority on the systems of relationship that structure church life offers in his last book a deeply human vision of community in which faith and hope can exist alongside the anxiety of these times. This book is a gift." —Rev. Stephanie Paulsell, Harvard Divinity School, author of *Religion Around Virginia Woolf*

"Here's a book that sheds light on the puzzle presented by troubled congregations. Steinke's insights from the theory of family systems lead clergy and laity to deeper understanding and discernment rather than to easy answers and quick fixes."
—James B. Brown, bishop, Episcopal Diocese of Louisiana

"Steinke is a clear-eyed, skilled consultant whose insights have stood the test of time. Other than Edwin Friedman, Steinke, a Lutheran pastor who studied with Friedman, is perhaps the most well-known of all practitioners of family systems theory." —*The Presbyterian Outlook*

The first edition of *How Your Church Family Works* was written nearly thirty years ago, and the reach and velocity of change in the past three decades pose a new challenge for churches. Thirty years ago, churches functioned in a fairly stable environment and focused on growth and expansion. The tide has turned now, though, and supplanted increase with decline. Bowen family systems theory—on which *How Your Church Family Works* is based—has not changed, but its application must be revised for the twenty-first century.

How Your 21st-Century Church Family Works, the second edition of Peter L. Steinke's landmark book, addresses the landscape of church sustainability with new introductory and concluding chapters bookending updates throughout the now-classic text. *How Your 21st-Century Church Family Works* embraces the anxiety caused by change, transforming it from a source of anguish to a font of opportunity.

Peter L. Steinke was an internationally recognized leadership consultant who served as a parish pastor, therapist, director of a counseling center, educator, and executive director of Healthy Congregations.

ROWMAN & LITTLEFIELD | 800-462-6420 | www.rowman.com

ISBN 978-1-5381-4913-3

9 781538 149133   90000

Cover image © Rawpixel/iStock/Getty Images Plus

P9-DBG-236